ethics
and public policy

public affairs and administration
(editor: James S. Bowman)
garland reference library
of social science
(vol. 414)

the public affairs and administration series: James S. Bowman, editor

ethics
and public policy

an annotated bibliography

Peter J. Bergerson

Garland Publishing, Inc. • New York & London
1988

Library of Congress Cataloging-in-Publication Data

Bergerson, Peter J., 1943–
 Ethics and public policy : an annotated bibliography / Peter J.
Bergerson.
  p.   cm. —(Public affairs and administration ; vol. 20)
(Garland reference library of social science ; vol. 414)
 Bibliography: p.
 Includes index.
 ISBN 0-8240-6632-4 (alk. paper)
 1. Political ethics—Bibliography. 2. Political ethics—United
States—Bibliography. I. Title. II. Series: Public affairs and
administration series ; 20. III. Series: Garland reference library
of social science ; v. 414.
Z7161.A15B47 1988
[JA79]
016.172—dc19   87-32997
                                                              CIP

Printed on acid-free, 250-year-life paper
Manufactured in the United States of America

to Catherine and Chris, and of course
Connie, who provided the inspiration
and encouragement

contents

series foreword

The twentieth century has seen public administration come of age as a field of study and practice. This decade, in fact, marks the one hundredth anniversary of the profession. As a result of the dramatic growth in government, and the accompanying information explosion, many individuals—managers, academicians and their students, researchers—in organizations feel that they do not have ready access to important information. In an increasingly complex world, more and more people need published material to help solve problems.

The scope of the field and the lack of a comprehensive information system has frustrated users, disseminators, and generators of knowledge in public administration. While there have been some initiatives in recent years, the documentation and control of the literature have been generally neglected. Indeed, major gaps in the development of the literature, the bibliographic structure of the discipline, have evolved.

Garland Publishing, Inc., has inaugurated the present series as an authoritative guide to information sources in public administration. It seeks to consolidate the gains made in the growth and maturation of the profession.

The Series consists of three tiers:
1. core volumes keyed to the major subfields in public administration such as personnel management, public budgeting, and intergovernmental relations;
2. bibliographies focusing on substantive areas of administration such as community health; and
3. titles on topical issues in the profession.

Each book will be compiled by one or more specialists in the area. The authors—practitioners and scholars—are selected in open competition from across the country. They design their work to include an introductory essay, a wide variety of biblio-

graphic materials, and, where appropriate, an information resource section. Thus each contribution in the collection
provides a systematic basis for managers and researchers
to make informed judgments in the course of their work.

Since no single volume can adequately encompass such a
broad, interdisciplinary subject, the Series is intended as a
continuous project that will incorporate new bodies of literature as needed. Its titles represent the initial building blocks in
an operating information system for public affairs and administration. As an open-ended endeavor, it is hoped that not only
will the Series serve to summarize knowledge in the field but
also will contribute to its advancement.

This collection of book-length bibliographies is the product
of considerable collaboration on the part of many people. Special appreciation is extended to the editors and staff of Garland Publishing, Inc., to the individual contributors in the Public
Affairs and Administration Series, and to the anonymous re-
viewers of each of the volumes. Inquiries should be made to
the Series Editor.

James S. Bowman
Department of Public Administration
Florida State University

preface

Political scandals over the past ten years have brought an outpouring of academic and popular research devoted to the analysis of ethics. Recent ethical questions surrounding the sale of military equipment to Iran and the cryptic funding of the Contra rebels in Nicaragua has brought ethics and government into public focus. My interest in this topic was stimulated while serving as secretary to the Professional Standards and Ethics Committee of the American Society of Public Administration.

This manuscript has been developed as a response to an academic need to provide a coherent ordering for an important body of literature. This text will provide a valuable reference guide to those who wish to educate themselves about ethics and public policy. Furthermore, it will be useful for academicians and administrators who are inquisitive about the field.

This manuscript has several noteworthy features. First, the book helps refine the primary issues in this area. Second, the bibliography provides a comprehensive and exhaustive list of articles published over the past 25 years. Furthermore, a classification system is developed to order the literature. Finally, a wide variety of issues is addressed.

This bibliography represents a comprehensive search of the scholarly literature in the field of ethics and public service. The bibliography was generated through an extensive computer search of eleven academic indexes using *Dialog*, an information retrieval service. This included the *American History and Life Database*, the *Congressional Information Service Database*, *Dissertation Abstracts*, *PTS Federal Index Database*, *Legal Resources Index Database*, *Public Affairs Information Service*, *Sociological Abstracts*, and *United States Political Science Documents*. These indexes catalog the world's literature from the major economic, legal, historical, political, and sociological journals. For example, *Public Affairs Information Index* includes 1,200 journals and 8,000 non-serial publications, while *Legal Resources Index* includes 660 key law journals. These indexes produced over 600 journal articles, dissertations, monographs, and case studies from the United States and throughout the world.

In preparing this manuscript, the author incurs many debts that need to be acknowledged. I am grateful for the assistance received from Brian P. Nedwek, Saint Louis University, on a convention paper which provided substantial groundwork for this volume. I am indebted to the editors at Garland Publishing for their confidence and support of my work. James S. Bowman, series editor, has been a source of encouragement and wise counsel. Pamela Chergotis, managing editor, has been patient and understanding. I am also grateful for the financial support from Southeast Missouri State University. This project would not have been possible without the excellent support provided by the staff of Kent Library at Southeast Missouri State University. My graduate assistant, Marilyn Hicks, was instrumental in the preparation and gathering of the material. Debbie Devenport has done an outstanding job typing the manuscript, for which I am very appreciative. Any errors or omissions, of course, are solely my responsibility.

Peter J. Bergerson
Cape Girardeau, MO

foreword

Ethics in public life is a topic of increasing general as well as academic concern. As sensational news stories constantly remind us, the issue cuts across all sectors of society: government, business, the media, education, religion, the professions. In none of these areas is ethics more crucial than in public administration— the management of public policy.

During the 1980s, dozens of administrative officials have been indicted, questioned by Congressional Committees, or otherwise given wide public attention for influence peddling, misusing authority, or engaging in other questionable activities. Most of the American states have acted during the past decade to establish ethics commissions and several have enacted legislation to protect whistleblowers from punitive retaliatory actions. As an indicator of popular interest in the subject, *Time* in 1987 established a regular feature on ethics and published a special issue on the subject.

Yet administrative ethics remains a field which is neither clearly defined nor sharply differentiated. Scholars disagree widely on the scope and content of the subject. The National Association of Schools of Public Affairs and Administration urges its members to include ethics in their graduate public administration curricula, but surveys of syllabi and faculty from such programs reveal a tremendous diversity of practice. Some courses and texts focus on bureaucratic corruption while others emphasize values clarification, administrative discretion, the multiple responsibilities of public officials, or substantive policy issues such as abortion, poverty, and biomedical ethics. The field continues to evolve, as philosophers, policy specialists, public administrators, academics, professional associations, and public interest groups seek to provide the concept of administrative ethics with meaning, definition, and substance.

Peter Bergerson has performed a doubly valuable service in preparing this annotated bibliography on Ethics and Public Policy. First, he has provided a rich bibliographical resource which researchers, instructors, and practitioners should all find useful. This selection of references to books, articles, and doctoral dissertations on the subject is more extensive than any prior bibliography. It covers both procedural and substantive policy issues and includes numerous foreign and international topics as well as those concerned specifically with the United States.

Bergerson's second important contribution is his classification of the broadly diverse items in this bibliography. His introduction develops and elaborates on this classification and suggests a number of interesting observations and comparisons. He has thereby not only helped to provide some order and definition to the still chaotic field, but has also suggested directions for possible future research.

Bergerson makes no claims that his classification scheme is definitive or that his coverage is exhaustive of all of the relevant literature. The fluidity of the field and the very pace of publication of new articles on the subject would in any case make such claims very fleeting. But Bergerson can rightfully take credit for having produced a valuable resource work which is sufficiently extensive, thorough, and carefully annotated to serve as both a base and a stimulus for future work.

Peter Bergerson has brought both expertise and careful reflection to the task of preparing this annotated bibliography. I have greatly enjoyed working with him on the Committee on Professional Standards and Ethics of the American Society for Public Administration (ASPA). His work on the committee, including service in recent years as secretary, has involved him centrally in ASPA's efforts to define and encourage ethical administrative behavior. As chairperson of his academic department, as a consultant to local government on ethical issues, and as a professional colleague he demonstrates those personal qualities of honesty, integrity, fairness, and dedication which one might hope to find in all administrators.

When an earlier and shorter version of this bibliography was presented at the 1986 ASPA national meetings in Anaheim, I regarded it as one of the best papers of the conference and felt it to be of considerable potential value to anyone interested in the subject. The subsequent development of the work, including the careful annotation, has further enhanced its value and usefulness. I am delighted that the Garland series on Public Affairs and Administration is making this bibliography available to a wider audience of scholars, practitioners, and others interested in ethics in public policy.

William L. Richter
Kansas State University

Chapter I

Introduction

> The real challenge at this point, then, is to
> work toward identifying criteria and refining
> measures which capture the extent to which ethics
> play a role in our form of government. (Gunn,
> 1980; item: 299).

Recent social, economic, and political debates have aroused a substantial public interest in ethics and its role in government. The 1980's have been a decade in which ethics and public management have come to the forefront of public policy. A substantial academic interest has accompanied the outpouring of public interest on this topic. For academicians and administrators, ethics lie at the heart of public policy analysis and application. Policy professionals know that critical issues of government ultimately involve moral choices. The concern of this research is a systematic investigation into the nature and substance of ethics research in recent years. A review of the research indicated a disjointed body of literature in need of a coherent and cohesive framework for analysis. This book is an attempt to examine the literature and identify the major themes and directions of the scholarship.

The author initiated this project in quest for a greater understanding of the academic tradition of ethics and public policy. The nine areas used to classify the literature became a simple typology that was perceived to hold some organizational utility. The areas are: Ethics and State and Local Governments, Comparative Government and Foreign Policy, Health

Care/Medical/Bio-Scientific, Ethics and the Interrelationship of
Government and Business, Codes of Ethics for Policy Analysis,
Multiple Roles of Policy Analysts, Criteria for the Analysis of
Alternatives and Principles of Decision-Making, Case Study
Applications, and Competing Paradigms and Theoretical Frameworks.

Ethics and State and Local Governments

The literature search revealed a substantial interest in
ethics at the state and local levels of government. The author
identified 24 articles on this issue, over half of which have been
published since 1980. The articles reflect a wide spectrum of
scholarships including Ph.D. dissertations, law review articles,
empirical research as well as popular commentary. Four patterns
emerge from the research. One set of articles focused on
legislation or policy in a specific state. For example, Cooper
(1976; item: 3) and (1979; item: 4) address the Alabama model,
while Samad (1983; item: 17) discusses ethics and public policy
in Connecticut and Ohio respectively.

A second research approach was prescriptive in nature.
Scholars such as Arkes (1981; item: 2) and Long (1975; item: 12)
discuss ethics from a philosophical and theoretical basis. Their
research centers on the ideal ethical environment for government.
A third direction revealed in the literature was the application
and operationalization of codes of ethics by state agencies. For

example McDowell (1980; item: 13) and Keys (1984; item: 10) examine the role of ethics from a policy implementation and policy analysis perspective.

Fourth, the literature reveals a keen interest in ethics at the local level. Ammons and King (1984; item: 1), Belt (1981; item: 89), Kenny (1981; item: 9), Kotler (1975; item: 11), and Murphy (1977; item: 15) examine the dimension of ethics as it applies to the mayor, manager, and the climate of local public administration.

An article by Hays and Gleissner (1981; item: 8) represents the most succinct analysis of activities among the American states. The author surveyed the personnel directors and ethics commissions of the 50 states to identify the trends in the establishment and implementation of formal codes of ethics. They found that agency directors and program administrators are primarily responsible for the creation and the administration of their own codes. In addition, they found that most state ethical codes were negative in tone, and lack any disciplinary provision. They conclude that most state codes of ethics are symbolic rather than substantive in nature.

Comparative Government and Foreign Policy

The codification of administrative ethics from a comparative/foreign policy perspective presents an academic challenge. The scholarship in this area reflects a divergence of opinions within the international community on what, in fact, is meant by ethics and furthermore what it encompasses. For example, Muslims argued that ethics and values are essential parts of their total way of life, thus any discussion of ethics and public policy independent of their religious principles is irrelevant. Others contend that ethics are intertwined with a nation's mores. Still, others see ethics as the "Trojan Horse" for introducing the undesirable aspects of science and technology into traditional value systems. Additional problems concern those who advocate a strong public enterprise system versus those who support private enterprise economy.

The literature search produced fifteen articles on comparative and foreign policy. Callard (1953; item: 29) was one of the first to compare the administrative ethics of the United States, Canada and Great Britain. Secondly, religion, ethics and public policy is the theme of four articles. Zahrany (1983; item: 44), Saidi (1980; item: 37), Al-Buraey (1981; item: 26), and Costa (1979; item: 30) analyze the impact of religion on the management of public policy. A third approach was to examine the ethical dimensions of specific foreign policy issues. For example, Dyson (1981; item: 31), King (1984; item: 34) and Strah (1984; item: 39) investigated the ethical dimensions of human rights, political scandals, and the Nigerian/Biafra conflict.

Huddleston's (1981; item: 33) article presents the most cogent analysis of ethics from an international and comparative framework. He identified three patterns of administrative ethics. These included polity based, statist and transcendent ethics. According to the author, **polity** based ethics refers to values drawn from the beliefs of the political community. Countries such as Canada, Britain and New Zealand are examples of this model. The **statist** based ethics is principally associated with countries of Continental Europe. In this system, the state is seen as an organic whole, and its administrative institutions and thus, ethics are to express the values of the whole, not the preferences of dominant political or social groups. **Transcendent** ethics denotes an environment in which ethics are defined in terms of spiritual or religious values. Japan in the early 19th century is considered the classic example of this model.

Huddleston points out that ethical patterns do not occur randomly, but must be understood as systematic responses to social and political conflict. He suggests that there are wide differences in patterns of administrative ethics between nations, and that ethics reflect political change. As new groups rise to power, administrative ethics will be adjusted to protect and enhance group status.

Health Care/Medical/Bio-Scientific

The literature review emphasized that few, if any public policy issues in recent years have raised more controversy than the ethical dimensions of government action in the area of health care and scientific research. In the past twenty years national and state governments have entered an arena of public policy decision-making, which had been shaped primarily by the family or dominant religious values in society. Today, administrators are faced with policy decisions which raise substantial ethical questions such as: When is a person dead? What is the value of life? Should government prolong a life? In 1982, the President's Commission for the Study of Ethical Problems in Medicine and Bio-medical and Behavioral Research raised such pointed questions as: Should the government oversee genetic engineering that could alter the biological makeup of human beings? What is an adequate level of health care? At what point should we stop extending a life? Is it $50,000, $500,000, or $1,000,000?

The literature suggests three avenues of scholarship. The first is ethics, medicine, and health care. In this category researchers explored ethical questions such as the quality, quantity, and distribution of health care in our society. Other articles have examined physicians' Code of Ethics and the ethical implications of their fees. Additional research explored the questions of mental health care, public health, as well as the legal aspects of ethics and medicine.

A second area of research focused on the ethical issue of using human subjects as objects of research. Articles in this area examined the ethical and moral questions of abortion, mental retardation, population control, and in vitro fertilization. Reiser (1978; item: 79) and Broadnax (1975; item: 49) raise seering questions about administrative ethics and human experimentation.

A third direction in the literature focuses on the scientific research and bio-technological advances. Serious concern has been raised that science and bio-medical research is so advanced as to be able to change the future of mankind as we know it today. Dennis Gabor (1964; item: 60) referred to this as the power to "invent the future." Specific articles raised ethical questions concerning DNA research, genetic screening, gene splitting and enhancement, and anatomical transplants. Furthermore, the United States Supreme Court ruled in 1980 that new forms of life created in the laboratory may be patented. The ethical implications of these issues present a substantial challenge for an administrator working in this environment.

Ethics and the Interrelationship of Government and Business

Recent events, such as the highly publicized General Dynamics-Department of Air Force procurement scandal have raised questions about the commingling of business practices with the management of public policy. The literature suggests three areas of concern associated with ethics, business, and government policy. These include, (1) the philosophical basis of government economic policy, (2) the ethics of multi-national corporations, and (3) the ethical implications associated with the privatization of the public sector.

Although the major concern of economists remains the development of models to predict economic behavior, greater interest has been shown in the ethical implications of government economic policy. This avenue of academic inquiry recognizes the necessity for economic theory of value and ethics as a basis for constructing or preserving moral order (DeGregori, 1977; item: 93). Social critics have also questioned the ethical and moral direction of the government economic policy in an affluent society. The central focus of this argument centers on faith in the "natural laws" of economics and the market systems ability to allocate resources fairly.

A second area of inquiry has been the ethical practices of multinational corporations and the foreign policy decisions of the United States to legitimize their actions. Vogel (1979; item: 101) argued that multinational corporations have extended their influence over global allocations of economic resources previously associated only with empires. He contended that multinational corporations regularly engage in excessive and illegal involvement in the political processes of the U.S. and foreign countries. Vogel pointed out how the public policy of the United States has sanctioned the economic practices of multinational corporations which profit from the policies of authoritarian regimes such as in South Korea.

A third concern of researchers has been the ethical implications associated with the move toward privatization of the public sector. The issues raised by Sonnenfeld (1981; item: 100), Miller (1981; item: 99), and Leys (1968; item: 96) are the ethical principles and standards of businesses who are awarded monopolistic contracts. The concern of some administrators is that public sector ethical standards may become contaminated by the ethical practices which guide many businesses. Clark (1952; item: 91) was one of the first to explore private interests and the role of administrative ethics. He was concerned with the lack of high standards and ethical practices of public employees.

Codes of Ethics for Policy Analysis

There is a substantial amount of research which prescribes and describes standards of ethical behavior for public employees. In fact, the literature review indicated that the largest single category of articles (80) related directly to codes of ethics. These articles analyze codes from several perspectives. The last section of this book will examine the direction of this research.

One set of articles calls attention to the importance of an individual's ethics to the performance of public policy. Bailey's (1964; item: 109) essay on the individual's role in administrative ethics is considered a classic. He argued that administrators need the "correct mental attitudes" to ensure the success of public policy. Lawry (1979; item: 148) follows up on this theme of emphasis on the individual. Furthermore, Wakefield's (1976; item: 175) award-winning article stressed the need for administrators to internalize a commitment to moral government.

A second approach emphasized codes of ethics for specialists such as **city managers** (Scheiber, 1975; item: 168), **policy experts** (Benveniste, 1984; item: 112), **planners** (Howe and Kaufman, 1980-1981; item: 140), **government attorneys** (Shapiro, 1981; item: 18, and Murphy, 1983; item: 156), as well as **senior executives** (Rohr, 1980; item: 165). Benveniste (1984; item: 112) argued for code of ethics "which would include such issues as defining the responsibility of the expert, identifying unacceptable conflicts of interest, determining the expert's objections regarding secrecy and disclosure and developing standards for the process of decision making in emergencies."

A third area of research has been the development of codes of ethics for public administration education. Rohr (1976; item: 164) addressed the role of ethics in public administration curriculum. Embry (1984; item 130) outlined his course on ethics and public administration. He presented a "pedagogical, philosophical, political and psychological" approach to the teaching of administrative ethics. Bok (1976; item: 114) asked the question, "Can ethics be taught?," while Blake (1966; item: 113) asked "Should the role of ethics be absolute or relative?" Worthley and Grumet (1983; item: 177) contend that educators are teaching what can't be taught, and Armstrong and Graham (1975; item: 107) outline the ethical preparation needed for a career in public service.

A fourth approach has been the intramural debate within the discipline on what a code of ethics should include. The evolution of public service as a profession has brought with it the establishment of a code of ethics (Public Administration Review, 1953; item: 181; Public Management, 1975; item: 182; Sherwood, 1975; item: 169; and Riggs, 1982; item: 160). Finkle (1984; item: 294) outlines the efforts of the profession to seek legitimacy, self respect, and standards through the adoption of codes of ethics. Chandler (1983; item: 122) presents arguments for and against the ASPA code. Three arguments against the ASPA code are that they are (1) impractical, (2) procedural, and (3) too theoretical. The positive points he makes are that they (1) are objective, (2) provide moral reasoning, (3) provide a common set of values for administrators.

Multiple Roles of Policy Analysts

A rich variety of roles have been offered and described in the policy literature. Each role has implications for the "ethics" of the occupant. One role portrays administrative officials as **arbiters** among conflicting interests. Here, ethical issues revolve largely around questions of prudential decision-making. The central question is whether or not an administrator has acted in the public interest. One of the earliest discussions appeared in the immediate post-war period (Maass and Radway, 1949; item: 207).

Similar to the ombudsman literature, another role has been described as that of **guardian** of democratic principles. The focus is upon the protection and enhancement of channels of access to maximize participation by those excluded from the policy process (Gunn, 1980; item: 299).

A popular role conception is that of **whistleblower.** Much of the literature describes the clash between personally held values and those of the organization. Peters and Branch (1972; item: 211), among others, identify ethical issues as the focal point for mechanisms of social control. Whether internally generated values or superimposed sanctions are more determinative in shaping administrative behavior is debated. Glazer (1983; item: 205) provides an excellent description of ten cases across a variety of institutional settings.

Perhaps the most common role descriptions are those of **problem-solver**. Behavioral expectations are shaped by technical considerations. Thus, expertise in "solving" technical problems best describes the emerging policy analyst's role in a complex society. However, as Foster (1980; item: 203) suggests, contemporary technical experts are more likely to be used as advocates of a client's preference. Ethical issues emerge as similar to those described in the lawyer-client literature.

An administrator can occupy multiple roles simultaneously. Typical investigations have focused on scientists (Mitcham, 1977; item: 208), criminologists (Czajkoski, 1971; item: 198), governmental advisors (Thompson, 1983; item: 262), and among others, city managers (Kenny, 1981; item: 9). Much like the literature about program evaluators, issues tend to focus on conflicts of interest that result from multiple stakeholder positions.

Criteria for the Analysis of Alternatives and Principles of Decision-Making

A tradition is emerging that moves the dialogue on the criteria of evaluation and decision-making well beyond an "efficiency" model of policy analysis. Ethical and aesthetic dimensions (Sagoff, 1981; item: 256) have been added to renew the discussion and to expand the notion of administrative responsibility.

For policy evaluation, assessing the merits of some programs has historically involved using some variations of utilitarianism in the selection of criteria. While the efficiency criterion has been the hallmark for the evaluation of alternative causes of action, the recent literature has begun to describe a variety of criteria. Whether one alternative is more desirable than another may be assessed on the basis of political feasibility, legality, or among others, a sense of fairness or justice.

Anderson (1979; item: 223) has made a strong case for expanding the basic principles used in policy analysis to include authority, justice, and efficiency. The justifiable exercise of power, i.e., authority, sets the stage for endless discussions about a public interest criterion in analysis and decision-making (Schubert, 1957; item: 257; Lilla, 1981; item: 246). Notions of justice provide a conceptual hook for the emerging issues of distributional consequences, e.g., problems of equity and equality (Chitwood, 1974; item: 228; Hart, 1974; item: 243; Grofman, 1981; item: 242; Porter and Porter, 1974; item: 252; and Lineberry and Welch, 1974; item: 247).

The efficiency criterion has been discussed recently as something other than an unbiased tool for decision-making. There is a growing awareness of the strong normative bias that undergirds the basic methodology, e.g., that operational definitions of benefits and costs are not apolitical. The normative bias goes well beyond the problem of which benefits to maximize. For example, risk management public administrators know only too well the bias inherent in the compensation schedules for accidental death or dismemberment.

When policy analysis is in other than an evaluative mode, ethical issues remain. Whether the activity is to predict future states of affairs, or to collect basic factual data on the causes and consequences of policy alternatives, ethical and moral forces are evident. In the area of planning and forecasting, Wachs (1982; item: 265) has warned us how technical objectivity in our prediction models can masquerade as an unbiased methodology.

The collection and analysis of policy-relevant data have been areas of ethical concern. Some research has focused on the criteria by which social experimentation involving human subjects is conducted (Thompson, 1981; item: 262). The development of criteria by which we initiate or terminate social experiments has been problemmatic. Others have examined the conduct of inquiry from the fact—value point of reference that appeared early in the literature (Simon, 1944; item: 258; Subramaniam, 1963; item: 260). Other ethical issues surrounding research have been discussed in the context of nonpositivist methodologies. For example, whether ethnographic sketches are subject to rules about freedom of the press, or whether ethnographic or anthropological notes can be subpoenaed, have been emerging issues.

Case Study Applications

The literature abounds with rich illustrations of ethical considerations in specific settings. Illustrations include immigration policy, capital punishment, abortion, legislative staff performance, and among others, the ethics in government legislation.

While specific events, e.g., Watergate, have generated case studies (Sundquist, 1974; item: 278), a variety of policy areas have been used to describe ethical issues. Twenty-two cases intended to develop analytical skills in public policy issue identification have been collected for dissemination (Dryfoos, 1984; item: 271).

Other than pedagogical applications, case studies have appeared to describe official misconduct, illegal actions, and the like, of public officials. The Ethics in Government Act has received considerable attention in recent years (Walter, 1981; item: 281; Dann, 1980; item: 270; Jack, 1981; item: 273). One study specifically investigated the Special Prosecutor's office under the act (Bertozzi, 1980; item: 269).

Substantive applications have appeared in immigration studies (Hudson, 1984; item 272), capital punishment (Tifft, 1982; item: 279), abortion (Lake, 1982; item: 70), and among others, legislative staff behavior (Kent, 1983; item: 275).   By and large, individual case studies have taken the form of a description of the personal ethics of public officials.   The common undercurrent is whether or not decision-makers are in conformance with a set of social norms that are prevalent in the policy arena under investigation.

Whether for pedagogical or analytic purposes, most of the case studies are limited to a sort of "conscience raising" activity.   As true of most case studies, the analysis tends to be highly idiosyncratic and difficult to induce basic principles or commonalities.

Competing Paradigms and Theoretical Frameworks

One of the more complex fields of the policy and ethics literature concerns competing paradigms and alternative theoretical frameworks.   The relationship between ethics and policy analysis has taken a variety of forms ranging from independence to complete integration.   A few bibliographic resources have chronicled the emerging competing views (Dunn, 1983; item: 290 MacRae, 1976; item: 308; Nagel, 1982; item: 312).

The classic view of ethics was strongly influenced by the scientific value relativism that permeated the early thinking and training in the social sciences.   Values were analytically separated from facts.   The latter were seen as the domain of the policy analyst, while the former were limited to "personal" policy analysis. Simply stated, only the question of what is policy in a specific arena was a proper query for the analyst. What should be the policy was a question of personal moral conviction.

As discussed in the section on the multiplicity of roles, a technocratic role orientation emerged to quard against the intrusion of values and moral questions in analysis. In a sense, ethical analysis was relegated to personal policy analysis. This rather doctrinaire separation of means and ends was a comfortable fit for a Weberian style of social science inquiry.

The value neutrality position became unacceptable among policy sensitive ethicists. Studies began to appear that questioned the value neutrality in policy analysis (Brown, 1978; item: 284). From problem specification through the techniques of analysis, the literature began to record the normative bias in much policy research. Ladd (1973; item: 304) noted that the dichotomization of means and ends distorted our conception of ends and blinded analysts to the values implicit in various techniques. Several analysts began to call for the explication of the normative assumptions in policy research (Amy, 1984; item: 106).

Renewing attention to policy goals in analysis provided an opportunity to grapple conceptually with the integration of problem analysis and ethical principles. MacRae (1975; item: 307) among others, suggested that normative analysis was as demanding as traditional empirical efforts and that "valuative" dependent variables be included in research.

Regardless of the set of preferred ends or principles, e.g., justice (Rawls, 1971; item: 317), the disparate activities performed by applied social scientists under the banner of policy analysis are ultimately drawn to the problem of choices. When the concerns are largely theoretic problems, the choices are from among competing explanations of either the causes or consequences of policy. Moreover, when analysts are interested in a more Lasswellian position, the choices are made among competing policy knowledges.

It is the political policy analyst (Bardes and Dubnick, 1980; item: 282) who focuses upon value maximization. Here, the analyst is thrust into an historically uncomfortable advocacy position. The diversity of these roles, institutional pressures on decision-makers, and competing ideological views suggests a more pessimistic assessment (Amy, 1984) that policy analysis and ethics are incompatible.

Summary and Observation

We have briefly reviewed the contributions to the literature on ethics in nine areas. Each section has suggested differing research traditions, goals, and related methodologies. In the State and Local area, some attention is given to ideal legislative initiatives; the tenor of the words is more prescriptive and finds expression in codes of conduct.

The comparative literature reflects highly divergent research interests. For some, ethics is part of an all-encompassing socio-political or religious belief system (or at least should be); for others, administrative ethics is a reflection of political change.

Health care ethical issues have become very salient in the past fifteen years. Some interest is focused on the distribution of health services, the morality of human service, or the emergence of scientific research and bio-technical consequences.

Governmental linkages to the private sector have provided opportunities to explore such diverse topics as the ethics of multinational corporations, the capacity of economic markets to allocate resources, or the privitization of public services.

The literature abounds with a variety of role descriptions of policy analysts and public administrators. Each role orientation appears to generate a set of distinctive ethical issues for the incumbent.

The generation of policy alternatives or criteria by which public decisions are made is an area highly reflective of the evolution of the study of public affairs. Born of utilitarianism, contemporary policy analysis is under pressure to expand the set of decision criteria to include other than "efficiency" elements.

Additional principles offered in the literature include justice, authority, and among others, legality.

One literature tradition, the case study applications, continues to provide a wealth of pedagogically useful material. Applications for ethical analysis have appeared in a variety of areas from administrative misconduct to specific policy areas. However, it remains uncertain whether or not these devices influence the behavioral skills of trainees.

The last literature area reviewed reflects a complex set of forces that are shaping the evolution of the public policy and administration field. Major paradigmatic pressures have led to the emergence of competing views of the goals of policy research and administration.

In sum, this literature review suggests the following:

1. While there are some exceptions (Howe and Kaufman, 1983; item: 301), the study of ethics has lacked an empirical approach; more often than not, studies are either highly prescriptive or normative, if not ideological;

2. Despite the numerous descriptive studies of ethics legislation, little attention has been given to a systematic analysis of the effects of ethics laws;

3. Overall, the area calls for increased analytic rigor through the expanded use of systematic investigations; and

4. The field of ethical investigations appears to run hot and cold in the literature. When it's hot, legislative initiatives and codes of ethics appear to satisfy the public clamor for responsible public officials. The study of ethics then, is perhaps better described as episodic in character, not institutionalized in any systematic manner. The study of ethics remains at a political level.

As Dunn (1983; item: 291) remarked:

> As policy analysis abandons its ethical innocence in the face of this normative complexity, we are faced, still, with the challenge of enlarging ethical knowledge through improvements in the methodology and practice of policy analysis.

Sources of Additional Information

The American Society for Public Administration has taken the lead in providing a forum for debate and discussion as well as a source of additional information on ethics and public policy. The Professional Standards and Ethics Committee of the Society is actively involved in the promotion of ethics. Budd Kass, a committee member from Eastern Washington State University, chairs a project entitled "Ethnet," which includes a comprehensive list of academicians and administrators who are interested in ethics and public management. Bayard Catron, George Washington University, Washington, D.C., publishes a newsletter devoted to news and information on ethics. Judith Truelson, Southern

California University, has done extensive work on a whistle-blower

information   project.   Kathryn   Denhardt,   University   of

Missouri-Columbia, is heading up a project on ethics education

which includes course syllabi and readings.

An additional source of information is COGEL, the Council on

State Governmental Ethics Laws. This organization's sole purpose

is to provide professional assistance to individuals and agencies

with responsibilities in governmental ethics, elections, campaign

finance, and lobby law regulation. COGEL is a clearing-house for

ethics information and publishes a quarterly newsletter. Their

address is P.O. Box 11910, Ironworks Park, Lexington, KY 40578.

Chapter II

Ethics and State and Local Governments

1. Ammons, David N., and Joseph C. King. "Local Government
   Professionalism." Bureaucrat 13, 2 (Summer 1984) 52-57.

   The authors pursue the notion of the status and
   development of professionalism in local government.
   Generally, local government conforms poorly to traditional
   criteria of professionalism. For example, public health
   professionals, city and county engineers, CPAs, police,
   generalist managers, administrative assistants, and budget
   officers are discussed. More importantly, the issues of
   professionalism are reviewed: professional autonomy,
   administrative excellence, the importance of graduate
   degrees, standards and the setting of them, effectiveness,
   efficiency, and the ultimate goals of professionalism.

2. Arkes, Hadley. The Philosopher in the City. Princeton:
   Princeton University Press (1981).

   This book is a blending of the philosophic and the
   political. The author argues to students that urban problems
   cannot be understood without an appreciation for
   political theory. Arkes states that moral judgments can be
   made only with principles of judgment. The author uses case
   studies based in Chicago to test our understanding of the
   principles of moral judgment. Immanuel Kant is used to
   interpret the actions of Mayor Daley.

3. Cooper, Melvin G. "The Alabama Ethics Act: Its Scope and
   Implementation." National Civic Review 65, 2 (1976)
   70-74.

   During the past few years and particularly after
   Watergate, there has been a renewed interest in political
   ethics at every level of government. National events have
   raised serious doubts as to the standards of conduct observed
   by elected officials. This has compelled many states,
   Alabama among them, to create such standards through
   legislation or executive order.

4. Cooper, Melvin G. "Administering Ethics Laws: The Alabama
   Experience." National Civic Review 68, 2 (1979) 77-81.

   The reason 40 or more states have passed ethics laws
   during the past few years is the undermining of the trust of
   the citizens by corrupt behavior on the part of a few
   officials at every level of government. Discusses not
   outright bribery or thievery, but rather a total lack of

ethical standards where a separation of public
responsibilities and private business interests are involved.
The amendments of 1975 weakened the law, but the "removal of
many of the overkill provisions made it far easier to
administer and implement." Chief Justice Warren said in 1962
"that such laws cannot be effective unless there is law
behind the law, i.e. an ethical concept on the part of all
those who accept public responsibilities."

5. Davis, I. Ridgway. "New Connecticut Code Reforms Lobbying
   Regulations." National Civic Review 69, 8 (September 1980)
   442-447.

   The 1979 Connecticut code of ethics is discussed in
   detail. It requires greater disclosure of lobbying
   activities and identification of lobbyists. The code was
   amended in 1979, effective January 1, 1980. Although it is
   still too soon to assess the effect of the legislation,
   overall expenditures have increased to over one million
   dollars in 1978. The number of registered lobbyists has also
   grown, from 392 in 1969 to 528 in 1978. The gambling lobby
   has developed into a strong organization during this period.

6. Fairbanks, David. "Politics, Economics, and the Public
   Morality: Why Some States are More Moral than Others."
   Policy Studies Journal 7, 4 (Summer 1979) 714-721.

   This research addresses the question of why some states
   attempt to be more moral than others in public policy.
   Morality policy and legislation in relation to birth control,
   divorce, gambling, and liquor is reviewed, determining each
   state's morality scale scores through simple correlation
   coefficients between morality policy scores and various
   religious, cultural, economic, and political variables.
   Findings showed that the best predictors of the type of
   morality of a state's public policy are religious beliefs and
   religious culture. Economic factors were not important
   determinants; political factors were seen as intervening
   variables.

7. Hammersmith, Stephen M. "Firm Disqualification and the
   Former Government Attorney." Ohio State Law Journal 42
   (Fall 1981) 579-602.

   This article analyzes the ethical standards of government
   attorneys who make the transition from public service to the
   private sector. Hammersmith focuses on the case of Armstrong
   vs. McAlpin from the 2nd Circuit of the U.S. Court of Appeals

in which the court reversed an earlier court decision by stating that an entire law firm did not have to be disqualified from participation in a case because one of its attorneys had substantial responsibility for the matter during his former employment. This article addresses a number of important ethical issues for attorneys, as well as the legal profession.

8. Hays, Steven H., and Richard R. Gleissner. "Codes of Ethics in State Government: A National Survey." Public Personnel Management Journal (1981) 48-58.

The authors discuss the current "state of the art" in ethics legislation. The objective is to describe the ethics practices in the fifty states and to identify major trends in the administration enforcement and content of formal codes of ethics. The research included a mail survey to all state personnel departments and ethics commissions. The authors found that ethics codes tend to be negative in tone, absent of disciplinary proceedings, and overwhelmingly complicated.

9. Kenny, Gerard Joseph. California City Managers: Policy Leaders or Political Dinosaurs. Ph.D. Dissertation, Claremont Graduate School, (1981).

Contrary to the Managers Code of Ethics, the fact that today's city manager is a policy-maker, a policy leader, and an active member in the policy process has been well established and widely accepted by the students and contemporary writers in their study of council-manager government. However, the question of the city manager's political involvement in attempting to implement policy has not been resolved and continues to be a source of contention in the relationship with the mayors and city council members.

This study assesses the policy and political role of the city manager as it pertains to the enigma of council-manager relationship, manager-community involvement, manager role perception, and the viability of council-manager government in today's complex society. Is the council-manager government viable or marasmic? Has this form of government reached that delicate balance between intransigence and subrogation? Can the perceived policy/political contentiousness between manager and council be ameliorated or will it eventually lead to the extinction of the council-manager form of government as we know it today? These are questions that this study analyzed from responses to a questionnaire sent to a sampling of California managers and mayors.

10. Keys, David Lee. North Dakota's Garrison Diversion Unit: A
Case Study of Domestic and International Environmental
Values Conflict. Ph.D. Dissertation, Indiana University,
(1984).

Initially, the GDU was to irrigate 1,007,000 acres in
North Dakota, but due to soil structure problems the project
was scaled down to 250,000 acres in the 1965 reauthorization.
Construction on the GDU began in 1968 with the Snake Creek
Pumping Station and is currently about 25 percent complete.
There are domestic environmental and economic troubles
plaguing the GDU such as wetland preservation and low
benefit-cost ratio. International problems are manifesting
themselves in the form of water quality and biota transfer
issues in the Canadian Province of Manitoba.

The research shows that from a deontological normative
perspective the U.S. is obligated by the Boundary Waters
Treaty of 1909 and its own Constitution to alter the GDU so
that Canada is not damaged environmentally or economically by
the GDU. The research also indicates that the candidate
theory of complex interdependence and its assumptions are
operative in the GDU controversy. The GDU closely fits the
candidate theory of complex interdependence and it can help
explain how and why the two countries have reacted to the GDU
controversy. The case also shows that the different values
the various actors bring to the decision-making process are
as important as the facts which they agree on or disagree
over.

11. Kotler, Milton. "The Ethics of Neighborhood Government."
Social Research 42, 2 (Summer 1975) 314-330.

Examined is neighborhood government. Assembly-based
neighborhood government by itself will not ensure happiness.
There are 3 directions of neighborhood government: (1) one's
own well-being, (2) the well-being of others, and (3) good
actions that please God. An attempt is made to show how good
neighborhood government promotes good will benevolence.
Those ideas dealing with good actions to oneself and to God
are not discussed here. There are proximate and distant
neighbors who deserve good will equally. There is no
institution that promotes the ideas of neighborly good will.
(Except possibly those places with the town meeting form of
government.) In the neighborhood governments, one must guard
against those who are out for power or their own gain. "The

exercise of power brings out the worst in man." While religion establishes ethical belief, good government and good laws are necessary to good will and benevolence. It is equally the duty of the neighborhood government to serve those in proximity and those far away.

12. Long, Norton E. "Ethos and the City: The Problem of Local Legitimacy." Ethnicity 2, 1 (1975) 43-51.

The author speculates on the importance of ethos and ethical structure in local government, asserting that shared ethos is necessary for harmonious governing and successful promotion of shared life-styles.

He begins this article by stating the Aristotelian concept of the state as the encompassing human institution designed to realize the good life for its citizens. In order for this to occur there must be some common conception of what the good life entails.

Long states that the free market and civil liberties play a role in the lack of social control and suggests that freedoms and constraints should be weighed against the valued concrete consequences of a particular course rather than against abstract conception of freedom. He then reviews: (1) social control achieved by modern ethnic and religious groups within cities and by cities in history; (2) the role of state and federal government in solving the problems of cities; and (3) the role of education in the breakdown of a common ethos. He concludes the article by indicating that the prospect of cities with powerful governments which can mobilize the latent forces within is frightening to those who see cities as social democratic threats to laissez-faire and to strong central government, but that without a strong local normative order the nation-state is weakened.

13. McDowell, Doris Marie. A Study of State Boards of Nursing in the United States: Board Members and Executive Directors. Ed.D. Dissertation, University of Kentucky (1980).

The purpose of this study was to examine the functions of state boards of nursing in the United States and to determine the extent of agreement between the views of the executive directors of boards of nursing and those of members of these boards as to their respective roles and each other's roles, and how these views coincide with ideal theoretical roles set forth by authorities.

The researcher developed a list of fifty-five postulates pertaining to the role of the executive officer, the role of board members, and the functioning of boards as the literature was reviewed. From the list of fifty-five postulates a ninety-nine item, two-part survey instrument was developed. Each of the two parts of the instrument included items on boards, board meetings, board members, and executive directors.

Based on the findings of the study, it was concluded that: (1) The majority of nursing boards operate in the periphery of state government rather than as an integral part of the organizational structure. (2) Executive directors of boards of nursing are state employees but do not enjoy all of the benefits of other state employees. (3) Demographic characteristics of some boards of nursing are not conducive to effective board functioning. (4) Membership is non-restrictive on some boards of nursing. (5) All board members do not resign their positions as officers in professional organizations when they are appointed to board membership. (6) Most boards provide an orientation program for their new board members. (7) Rudimentary procedures for conducting a business meeting are not practiced during some board meetings. (8) Most of the boards of nursing do not use standing committees. (9) Board members receive compensation for their services as board members. (10) Boards of nursing have not defined the role and responsibilities of their executive directors or their own role as board members. (11) The evaluation process of executive directors and board activities lack purpose and regularity. (12) Boards of nursing do not have a written code of ethics for its own members' behavior.

14. Mullins, Phil, Thomas O. Leatherwood, and Arthur Lipow, (ed.). Political Reform in California: Evaluation and Perspective. University of California, Berkeley, CA (November 1975).

This book relates the efforts of a coalition of political reformers to "put an end to corruption in politics" in California. The individuals reflected diverse groups who sensed a wide spread frustration with politics and government. The reformers lead a drive for a state-wide initiative. This book is an excellent example of direct democracy in action. The successful efforts lead to the California Political Act of 1974.

15. Murphy, Thomas P. "Ethical Dilemmas for Urban
    Administrators." Urbanism Past and Present 4 (Summer
    1977) 33-40.

    The author discusses ethical dilemmas that urban
administrators in the U.S. are often faced with and
alternative ways of dealing with such situations. These are
situations in which governmental decisions involve ambiguous
legal and moral considerations. Two specific types of
situations are considered: 1) When the public official has
the opportunity to obtain personal profit because of his
access to inside knowledge; and 2) Dealing with political
pressure for job hiring. The author then explores the
ethical considerations related to two different approaches to
governmental administration: 1) Advocacy approach, which
sees the role of the urban administrator as not just
administering the laws impartially, but making positive
efforts to change the laws so they better meet the needs of
the public; 2) The traditional approach, which emphasizes
efficiency and sees the role of the administrator as simply
impartially administering policies set by others. Several
court cases arising from the activities of different advocacy
groups are described as the author shows how the advocacy
approach provides administrators with a basis for making
organizations adopt ethical standards as policy. Noting that
organizations have usually responded to dilemmas of ethical
choice by establishing guidelines governing their members'
behavior, the author suggests that this is insufficient and
more is needed, such as the administrators making a personal
commitment to high standards of professional ethics.

16. Patriarche, John M. "Ethical Questions Which Administrators
    Face." Public Management 57, 6 (June 1975) 17-19.

    Specific examples of ethical dilemmas for city managers,
such as conflict of interest because of property ownership or
acceptance of gifts, with suggestions for avoiding these
problems.

17. Samad, Stanley A. "Ohio Revised Rules for the Government of
    the Judiciary and the Bar: A Critique." Capital
    University Law Review 13 (Fall 1983) 25-39.

    In this article the author outlines the changes in the
Ohio Judicial Code of Conduct both for lawyers and judges.
The objective of this revision was to enhance public
confidence in the legal profession and the courts. The
article focuses primarily on the new rules for the governing

of the Ohio Bar and the new standards for disciplinary action.

18. Shapiro, Stephen J. "Judicial Control over the Bar Versus Legislative Regulation of Governmental Ethics: The Pennsylvania Approach and a Proposed Alternative." Duquesne Law Review 20 (Fall 1981) 13-41.

In this article the author discusses developments relating to ethics laws, the Pennsylvania Courts, and conflicts with the state legislature. Pennsylvania's ethics legislation is the source of conflict between the legislature and judicial branches of government. This article outlines the problems associated with the ethics legislation and offers a compromise position. The conflict is centered on who is responsible for application of ethics legislation; the courts or the bureaucracy.

19. Terapack, Richard G. "Administering Ethics Laws: The Ohio Experience." National Civic Review 68, 2 (1979) 82-84.

More than 40 states have passed some form of ethics legislation since the beginning of the 1970's. The reason is simple. Corrupt and unethical behavior on the part of a few officials at every level of government undermined the faith and trust of the citizens. Has the administration of those laws been effectively balanced or has it been marked by overkill? The latter did occur in Alabama due to amendments to the law made by the legislature. Ohio's track record is seen more on the balance side.

20. Vernon, George. "The Illinois Code of Professional Responsibility: A New Blueprint for Disciplinary Enforcement." De Paul Law Review 30 (Winter 1981) 365-401.

21. Woodard, J. David. "Ethics and the City Manager." Bureaucrat 13, 1 (Spring 1984) 53-57.

The article analyzes, from the perspective of a city manager, the 1924 code of ethics for the profession. The original code and subsequent revisions are based on the idea that administration could be and should be apolitical. In modern reality, the author contends, citizens in a community expect far more than apolitical idealism from their manager. In fact, they expect action and politics. The article provides suggestions for revising the code to include: 1) Recognition of the job's political dimension, and 2) Making the code shorter.

22. Young, William H. "Government, Mayors and Community Ethics."
     Annals of the American Academy of Political and Social
     Science 280 (March 1952) 46-50.

     The author believes that men rise to the office and its
     "awesome responsibility" and do not want to do wrong.
     Because of this "goodness" man can best influence others
     through exemplary leadership.

23. Zimmerman, Joseph F. "Municipal Codes of Ethics: A
     Commentary." National Civic Review 64 (December 1975)
     577-580.

     A relatively large number of statutes have been enacted
     over the years to promote public integrity by ensuring that
     private interests do not benefit unfairly from the operations
     of government. In recent years emphasis has been placed on
     legislatively enacted codes. Since 1970 in New York State
     every city, county, school district, village and town has
     been required to adopt and file such a code with the state
     Department of Audit and Control.

24. "Ethics in Local Government." Public Management 57 (June
     1975) 2-19.

     The entire issue is devoted to ethics and local
     government. It includes six articles authored by well-known
     academicians and administrators, such as Harland Cleveland,
     Mark E. Klane, Keith Mulrooney, Elmer B. Staats, and Frank
     Sherwood. The articles assess ethics following the Watergate
     Scandal, the ICMA Code of Ethics, and the ethical questions
     which administrators face. This volume gives an excellent
     overview of the issues and concerns facing city managers.

25. Selected Opinions of the State Ethics Commission.
     Pennsylvania Law Journal Reporter. 6 (January 24, 1983)
     2.

Chapter III

Comparative Government and Foreign Policy

26. Al-Buraey, Muhammad Abdullah. Administrative Development:
    An Islamic Perspective. The Possible Role of the
    Islamists in Development of the Muslim World. Ph.D.
    Dissertation, University of North Carolina at Chapel Hill
    (1981).

    This dissertation presents a developmental perspective
    different from the prevailing Western one. It is hoped that
    this point of view will contribute towards the goal of
    developing a general theory of world development of human
    societies that presently does not exist. Though the focus of
    the study is on Islamic views of administrative development,
    other aspects of development (such as political and
    socioeconomic) are also discussed.

    Most of the recent turmoil in the Muslim World points
    toward a direction upon which many Muslim intellectuals
    agree: a return to the basic and pure spirit of Islam as a
    natural phenomenon in the contemporary world is a viable
    alternative to the failure of Western models of development.
    The major theme is that Islamic models of administration will
    better achieve developmental goals than "Western" models.

    The study is divided into three major parts. In Part I,
    "The Ideology For Development," chapter 1 gives a
    comprehensive background and analysis of Islam, its various
    theories and related issues, as a guiding ideology for
    development. Chapter 2 discusses man and development and
    portrays an Islamic view of human nature. In Part II, "The
    Environment of Development," chapter 3 discusses political
    development; and chapter 4, socioeconomic development. Part
    III, "Administrative Development," is the core of the study
    and contains three chapters. Chapter 5 details the
    administrative sources in Islam and researches Islamic roots
    of administration. Chapter 6 analyzes the elements and
    dynamics of an Islamic model of administration with emphasis
    on its Six P's Version. Finally, chapter 7 outlines the
    strategy, implementation, and implications of this model,
    emphasizing the Islamist's role in the process. Brief
    concluding remarks, presenting a summary and the direction of
    future research, complete the study.

27. Arroyo, Miguel Gonzalez. The Making of the Worker:
    Education in Minas Gerais, Brazil (1888-1920). Ph.D.
    Dissertation, Stanford University (1982).

    This dissertation has attempted to advance our
    comprehension of the relationship between education and work

in a peripheral economy, that of Brazil. This period studied was limited to the phase of agro-export capitalist transition. One of the changes demanded during that transition was the transformation of labor into labor power, i.e., a change from slave labor, along with the attendant transformation of beliefs and values concerning work discipline. Turning ex-slaves, free workers and immigrants into wage laborers was a social, political and cultural problem for the Brazilian ruling class. Working people resisted this change, and their resistance was understood as political-cultural opposition to the ethics of free labor. The governing class and employers were cognizant of the solution to the problem, but still had to determine how the dominated class could best be educated to accept its social role in the labor system, and how the value-system of the working people could most effectively be altered.

28. Caiden, Gerald E.   "Ethics in the Public Service: Codification Misses the Real Target." _Public Personnel Management_ 10, 1 (1981).

The author reviews the efforts of the 1979 International Conference on the Improvement of Public Management in Washington, D.C. The theme of the conference was public service ethics and efforts to enhance the practice of ethical behavior. The discussions included common issues in public service responsibility, ethical predicaments facing civil servants, feasibility of ethical education and training, traditional values in curriculum design and approaches for training. Four major needs were identified: (1) to develop curriculum for training and education in ethics; (2) to consider the reform of public organizations aimed at minimizing the necessity for the exercise of ethical judgments; (3) to adopt and enforce statements of the standard of conduct normally required by civil servants; and (4) to impress on officials the importance of study and research into organizational arrangements to minimize opportunities for corruption.

29. Callard, Keith. "On the Ethics of Civil Servants in Great Britain and North America." _Public Policy_ 4 (1953) 134.

This article raises ethical issues about public service ethics in Western Democracies. He contends that the problems of ethical standards of public life are treated as a matter of adopting a new set of maximums and seeing that it is enforced. He draws on examples primarily from the U.S., Canada and Britain. He argues that the bureaucrat has to cultivate that 'bent of mind' which will guide his behavior. He suggests that the bureaucracy is likely to render better service to the community if it's allowed to develop some degree of professional autonomy.

30. Costa, Esdras Borges. Protestantism, Modernization and Cultural Change in Brazil. Ph.D. Dissertation, University of California-Berkeley (1979).

From the last quarter of the 19th century to the 1960's the major Protestant denominations in Brazil have grown from nothing to diversified religious bodies of regional or national geographic expansion and considerable institutional development. Organized Protestant communities can be found in rural and urban areas of all regions of the country.

Throughout the years of their expansion and development the Brazilian Protestant churches have often held the belief that a religion of conversion and righteous individual conduct and the principles and practice of liberal democracy are the foundations of a modern and good society. To express this stance they have faced ideological and practical problems. Some of such problems are reviewed in the present dissertation, in the context of four periods that are defined by reference to major trends of political change in the country and of internal development of Brazilian Protestantism. This descriptive review is organized around the following themes: (1) Formative Traditions in the History of Brazilian Protestantism (1860-1930). (2) Some Protestant Responses to the Expansion of the Modern State (1931-1945). (3) Protestantism and Religious "Internalization" in Times of Limited Democracy (1946-1960). (4) Responses to Modernization among Brazilian Protestants in the 1960's.

31. Dyson, Kenneth. "The Problem of Morality and Power in the Politics of West Germany." Government and Opposition 16 (Spring 1981) 131-148.

The focus of this article is the "morality" of abrasive and emotional electoral campaigns in West Germany. A lingering fear remains from the memories of the Weimar Republic and the Third Reich when elections were brutal. The question raised by the article is how moral standards like mutual respect are to be maintained during an election struggle in which personality and style of leadership would be the central issue. German political parties created a Schiedstelle: institutions designed to provide formal guarantees of civil behavior. This institution is to act as a neutral referee of the electoral struggle for power. Tentative reports from the 1980 election illustrated the effectiveness of this institution.

32. Garant, Patrice. "L'ethique dans la fonction publique." Canadian Public Administration 18, 1 (1975) 65-90.

33. Huddleston, Mark W. "Comparative Perspectives on Administrative Ethics: Some Implications for American Public Administration." Public Personnel Management 10, 1 (1981) 67-76.

This essay examines ethics from an international comparative perspective. The author addresses three issues, these include: (1) what are the major patterns of administrative ethics, (2) why do particular patterns develop, persist and change, (3) what do these developments imply for Public Administration in the U.S.? Huddleston concluded this essay with some practical implications for American administration: (1) he argues that ethics is not an issue of making administrations more ethical, but conforming to a different sort of ethics; (2) changes in ethical behavior on the part of public managers must be preceeded by changes in the ethical behavior of politicians; (3) an incentive system must be set up to encourage ethical behavior; (4) tension and conflict in Administration Ethics are endemic.

34. King, Anthony. "Transatlantic Transgressions: A Comparison of British and American (Political) Scandals." Public Opinion 7 (January 1984).

In this article the author reviews the numerous scandals that have rocked the British and U.S. governments over the past 30 years. King's essay, tongue in cheek, suggests a new academic subfield called "scandalology." He suggests that British scandals often involve sex while U.S. scandals often involve glory and power. King suggests that the U.S. may have more scandals than the British partly because they have higher ethical standards than the British.

35. Oguah, Benjamin E. "African and Western Philosophy: A Comparative Study." Journal of African Studies 4, 3 (Fall 1977) 281-295.

In this article the author compares the philosophical

ideas of the Fanti of Ghana with those from Western
philosophy. He states that: 1) Fanti metaphysical
philosophy is a version of Cartesian dualism and body-soul
interactionism; 2) The same problem of other minds is found
in both philosophies; 3) Similar issues and doctrines are
found in Fanti and Western philosophical theology--the
ontological argument, the cosmological argument, the
teleological argument, the problem of evil, and immortality;
4) The Fanti believe in innate ideas, and there is both
belief and skepticism about extrasensory perception. The
Fanti differ from Westerners in some philosophical areas: 1)
The Fanti system of ethics is anti-egoistic (the good of the
individual is seen as a function of the good of society); 2)
Punishment for a crime is seen not only as a deterrent and a
means for exacting restitution, but also as an opportunity to
purify the offender and to rid him of his guilty feelings; 3)
Fanti political philosophy rejects both socialism and
capitalism in favor of libertarian basicalism, in which
government is both the legal and the economic custodian of
society and the basic necessities of life are provided freely
for all in a free society. The author states that the
philosophical ideas of the Fanti are reflected in the
philosophies of many other African societies.

36. Orr, G.S. "Ethics in the Public Service." New Zealand
     Journal of Public Administration 37 (March 1975) 1-7.

     An edited version of an address to the Civil Service
Institute in Wellington, New Zealand, stressing personal
examples by senior officials and loyalty to the Public
Service as more valuable than codes of ethics or personal
values for controlling behavior. Ethics must be in the
context of three recent developments. First, there is a move
toward more openness in government. Second, public servants
are much more visable, and enjoy greater public exposure.
Third, there are signs of a "double allegiance" emerging on
the part of some civil servants, between their professional
association, such as engineers, and loyalty to government.
This essay provides an excellent discussion of ethics from
the New Zealand perspective.

37. Saidi, Bijan. The Civil Service of Iran: Problems and
     Prospects. Ph.D. Dissertation, New York University
     (1980).

     Performance of civil service and public sector employees,
in large measure, determines the success of government action
for educational, social, and economic development. The

growth and expansion of governmental activities, improvement
in the performance of the public sector, the organization and
reorganization of the civil service and public sector
employees to attract, retain and make the best qualified
personnel, have remained the central concerns of states.

The purpose of this study is to examine the principles
underlying the public personnel system in Iran, and in
particular to what extent the basic concepts of the
humanistic school of management have been introduced and
implemented in practice in the course of the post-war period.

38. Schindler, Ruben. "Welfare and Work in Israel: A Case
    Study." The Social Service Review 55, 4 (December 1981)
    636-648.

The Protestant ethic deeply rooted in United States
society exemplified the relationship between work and
welfare. Social welfare policy in Israel has also been
influenced by social, political, and religious movements.
The strong tie between work policy in Israel has its roots in
the formative years of the nation, very much as United States
welfare policy is grounded in the values of the past. The
development of the ideological and philosophical roots of the
work ethic in Israel is discussed, along with its influence
on the social services in the period before statehood, and
its consequences for welfare policy in the period after
statehood, where it is reflected in the major trends of the
national insurance and welfare policies up to the present.

39. Strah, Michael Sherman. An Ethical Analysis of United States
    Involvement in the Nigerian/Biafran Conflict. Th.D.
    Dissertation, Boston University School of Theology (1984).

This dissertation attempts (1) to discover, and (2) to
evaluate from a particular ethical perspective, the nature
and extent of the United States' involvement in the Nigerian
Civil War. Data for the study are obtained from books and
articles, government documents declassified at the writer's
request, and interviews with government officials who
formulated the United States' response to the Nigerian
crisis.

The inquiry begins with the development of three
analytical tools: (1) an historical analysis of Nigeria's
development as a nation and the development of United States
foreign relations with Nigeria, (2) an analytical model of

international relations, and (3) an ethical perspective based upon H. Richard Niebuhr's ethics of universal responsibility and the concept of the responsible society. Critically, this perspective provides a basis for analyzing the concept of responsibility operative in the formulation of particular foreign policies. Normatively, it seeks to develop foreign policies guided by three major goals which the United States shares with other nations and to maintain, in the exercise of power in international relations, a careful balance among the requirements of freedom, justice, accountability, and order. Power controlled by these norms seeks to be universally responsible by enhancing the welfare of all those affected by its use. Consequently it is identified as "the responsible exercise of power."

40. Thompson, Kenneth W. Ethics and International Relations. Transaction Inc., New York (1985).

This book is an edited volume of ethics related articles based on the perspective of moral reasoning. This volume examines the relationships and interconnections between competing moral and political principles. It attempts to balance what is morally desirable with what is politically possible. The editor argues that a foreign policy for the nuclear age requires the developing countries to display moral and political discrimination and the balancing of competing military, political, economic and social objectives.

41. Thompson, Kenneth. "New Reflections on Ethics and Foreign Policy: The Problem of Human Rights." Journal of Politics 40, 4 (November 1978) 984-1010.

The author focuses on the conclusions reached by a conference (which included diplomats, theologians, and academicians) on human rights and international politics at the University of Virginia in June, 1977. Nations, especially the U.S., are wont to formulate and articulate foreign policy in moral terms. From the diplomatic perspective, there is evidence both of moral improvement and of moral decline in international politics. International lawyers, on the other hand, are inclined to apply more rigorous criteria in defining morally proper foreign policies. While diplomats emphasize workability when evaluating foreign policy, the legal community stresses abstract principle; and, where diplomats view the international environment as being constant in many ways, the lawyers emphasize and favor change. These two groups, as

well as theologians and spokesmen for the Third World,
believe that one cannot rely exclusively on governments to
promote a concern for human rights. The author concludes
with a commentary on Michael Howard's framework, which views
politics as two-dimensional and as involving ethics and power
as its co-ordinates, and its application to human rights.

42. Tickner, F. J. "Ethical Guidelines for Administrators:
    Comparison With Whitehall." Public Administration Review
    (November/December 1974) 587-592.

A description of the organizational structure and
procedures and public service traditions such as loyalty to
the monarchy which differ from characteristics of the U.S.
public service and lead to greater professionalization of the
British Civil Service. The author reflects on fifty years
with the British Civil Service. He argues that the British
Civil Service is motivated by loyalty to the monarch and a
sense of public service. The author presents an excellent
discussion of the ministerial responsibilities of the British
system and the twin loyalties of those who serve the crown
and the government.

43. Vaughn, Robert G. "Implications of the British Experience on
    Administrative Regulation of Conflicts of Interest in the
    Federal Civil Service." American University Law Review
    30 (Spring 1981) 705-729.

This article examines the British experience with an
ethical code for government officers and employees. In
particular, the article focuses on receipt of gifts and the
acceptance of outside employment by government employees.
The article also explores the more general implications of
conflict of interest regulation in the British Civil Service
level among employees of local government in Great Britain.
The author attempts to compare the British experience with a
similar code of ethics for U.S. civil servants. He found
that in Britain there is far greater attention given to
enforcement provisions of the ethics code.

44. Zahrany, Saleh Faris. Political Representation in Islam.
    Ph.D. Dissertation, Catholic University of America (1983).

Islam is indistinguishably a religion and a
socio-political community. According to the Islamic
conception, society should be constructed in accordance with
the Will of God, as expressed in the Shari'ah (the Koran and
the Sunnah, or the teachings of Muhammad). The Shari'ah is a

code of life that regulates every aspect of human existence.

The Shari'ah provides a broad constitutional framework for the Islamic state and is meant to be adapted to changing times. The adaptation of this constitutional framework to the needs of every age is incumbent upon every Muslim generation. Central to the Islamic constitutional framework is the principle of representation, including the principle of government by consent and consultation. However, the ideal of government by consent and consultation was realized in practice only under Muhammad and the four Khulufa (Caliphs) who succeeded him (1-40 A.H./661 A.D.).

To explicate and define the principle of representation this study analyzes the structure of the Shari'ah and the notion of state and government in Islam as envisioned in the Divine law and as exemplified by the constitutional practices of the early Muslims. It also examines the prominent place of ethics and scholarly knowledge in Islamic constitutional traditions.

Chapter IV

Health Care/Medical/Bio-Scientific

45. Barber, Bernard. "In Vitro Fertilization." National Forum
    69 (Spring 1979) 32-34.

    In vitro fertilization of human ova has been under
    discussion since the early 1970s, though public attention was
    first drawn to it with the impending birth of Louise Brown.
    This practice creates complex problems for public policy.
    The continuation of in vitro fertilization and implantation
    is desirable, given continuous monitoring of practitioners'
    activities. This monitoring will not be welcomed by
    researchers, but it is necessary to persuade the research
    community to accept it as an aspect of their acceptance of
    the obligations of biomedical ethics.

46. Barber, Bernard. "Perspectives on Medical Ethics and Social
    Change." The Annals of the American Academy of Political
    and Social Science 437, (May 1978) 1-7.

    Medical ethics are now in a period of great change. Some
    of the patterns, causes, agents, modes, resistance to, and
    costs of these changes are briefly described. Causes of
    change include technological determinism, rationality as a
    set of values, and egalitarianism as a set of values. Agents
    of change are insider medical professionals, (i.e.,
    "humanists," "bioethicists," social scientists, and some
    government people). Modes of change include social movement,
    legal action, and government policy. Laymen complain about
    the huge expense of medical aid; professionals complain about
    the decline of trust in their efforts. Slowly, too, medicine
    is losing some of its omnipotence in the community. As the
    process of change continues, perhaps even more quickly than
    in the last hurried fifteen years, it is hoped that there
    will be less conflict and more rational remedy.

47. Barber, Bernard. "Control and Responsibility in the Powerful
    Professions." Political Science Quarterly 993, 4 (Winter
    1978-79) 599-615.

    Professional activities involve: 1) important knowledge;
    2) autonomy; 3) public responsibility. Professional
    occupations in the United States are being attacked for
    irresponsibility, an inability to police themselves, and a
    refusal to permit nonprofessionals to participate in those
    professional decisions affecting lay persons. The author
    maintains that these attacks result from: 1) The increased
    power of the professions; 2) Changes in popular values.
    Examples of these problems in various professions (e.g.,
    medical malpractice and research, lawyers' insensitivity to

justice, ties between professional accountants and
corporations, and academic arrogance and dogmatism) are
discussed. It is likely that corrective efforts will come
from: 1) improved self-regulation; 2) public involvement;
3) governmental intervention. The author views the alleged
shortcomings of the professions as being social problems
requiring sociological analysis.

48. Berelson, Bernard, and Jonathan Lieberson. "Government
     Efforts to Influence Fertility." Population and
     Development Review 5 (December 1979) 581-613.

     After an outline of various problems posed by the growth
or decline of population and the feasible means available to
governments for dealing with them, the question is posed of
whether important ethical issues are raised by current
interventionist policies. These policy options are surveyed
and shown to fall into three categories of government
intervention: (1) limitations imposed on access to modern
methods of fertility control; (2) incentives and
disincentives of various kinds; and (3) politically organized
peer pressure. With regard to ethical issues raised by these
policies, the traditional procedure in the ethical literature
of first providing an over-arching ethical theory and then
deducing consequences pertaining to particular issues (in
this case population controversies) is inverted. Instead, a
contextual and piecemeal approach is adopted, which views
ethics as a species of decision making, resting on
agreed-upon premises and proceeding to substantive
conclusions as to what action should be taken in particular
situations. The three sets of policies are examined from
this perspective, and limitations on access and incentive
programs are found to be ethically permissible, provided
certain safeguards and intuitive conditions are satisfied.
Politically organized peer pressure is found unethical,
except under stringent conditions and where other approaches
have been tried first. Aspects of the ethical framework
underlying these judgments on the policy are clarified, and a
number of subsidiary problems are discussed.

49. Broadnax, Walter D. "The Tuskegee Health Experiment: A
     Question of Bureaucratic Morality?" The Bureaucrat 4
     (April 1975) 45-56.

     A case study illustrating the changing nature of social
values and how such change affects the bureaucracy. Stating
that racial attitudes were a decisive factor in the Public
Health Service's decision to withhold penicillin treatment

for a group of syphillis patients, Broadnax concludes that only external pressure resulting from media exposure and the more tolerant racial attitudes of the 1970s led to PHS acknowledgement of the injustice. He suggests that we have no guarantees that the dynamics of values will always be positive.

50. Caldwell, Lynton K. "Managing the Scientific Super-Culture: The Task of Educational Preparation." Public Administration Review (June 1967) 128.

This generation must assume the responsibility to control the forces of science and technology that human ingenuity has liberated. The rapid growth of our organizing and managing skills fails to pace the accelerating tempo of science and technology. Too few have sensed the true enormity of the impending managerial task. Furthermore, fewer have seen the urgency to control and direct the thrust of this scientific advancement. What is needed is a greatly enlarged, sustained, and self-critical effort to assess the managerial needs of the emergent super culture and to reinforce and expand the mid-career educational efforts already underway.

51. Callahan, Daniel. "Abortion and Medical Ethics." The Annals of the American Academy of Political and Social Science 437 (May 1978) 116-127.

Despite the Supreme Court decision in 1973, Roe v. Wade, making abortion legally available without impediment during the first two trimesters of pregnancy, neither the legal nor ethical problems of abortion have been solved. Congressional opposition to federal financial support of abortion, as well as a wide disparity in availability of abortion, indicates the still unsettled state of public policy on the issue. In medical ethics, a number of problems have surfaced in the past few years, which together form a complex set of both moral and legal issues. Fetal research, on the one hand, and the prospect of in vitro fertilization, on the other, both point to issues which recent Supreme Court decisions have not clarified. The rapid development of amniocentesis as a major tool of prenatal diagnosis highlights some of the new dilemmas. If the Supreme Court decision is read literally, there would appear to be no grounds for a physician to refuse to perform an abortion except for a clear threat to a woman's health from the abortion itself. Yet many, and perhaps most, physicians appear morally opposed to using abortion for sex selection or in those cases where simple postnatal treatment is available to correct a genetic defect. What are the

rights of physicians in such cases and what, if any, are the
limits on the rights of women to have abortions? Lurking in
the background is the growing power of medicine to push back
the time of viability of an infant earlier and earlier. Both
new legal and ethical problems are bound to result. Abortion
remains as deeply complex a moral issue as ever.

52. Callahan, Daniel. "Ethics and Population Limitation."
    Science (February 4, 1972) 487-494.

While in the past childbearing was uniformly assigned a
high social value, present conditions make unrestricted
population growth a source of grave dangers to the human
race. Formulation of policies requires 3 concerns: The ends
pursued, the means available, and the criteria for evaluation
of means and ends. The primary human values have been
freedom, justice, and survival; each can sometimes validly be
traded off for the others. The value of freedom implies that
childbearing is primarily a parental choice, subject to the
rights of others; government may intervene to protect these
rights, but must show clear danger to them. The most
questionable approach would be compulsory abortion and
sterilization after a given number of children; financial
penalties, or financial rewards for not bearing children are
less offensive, but violate justice by weighing more heavily
against the poor. In general, governments must first prove
that voluntary programs have been tried and have failed, and
that crucial human values are threatened by population
growth, to justify coercive measures, which even then can be
overthrown by demonstrations of severe harm to the crucial
human values; they are obligated to try the least coercive
policies first. This approach involves some risks, but any
view which gives primacy to free choice is risky; claims for
the reduction of rights must derive from other rights.

53. Clarke, Michael, and Patrick McInturff. "Public Personnel in
    an Age of Scientificism." Public Personnel Management 10,
    1 (1981) 83-86.

The main point of this essay is to indicate that the legal
tradition no longer provides an adequate safeguard against
public corruption. Further, the author suggests, the broad
outlines of a paradigm of government ethics, based on a
clearer understanding of the public interest, is beginning to
emerge. In this article a new model, based on the value of
human worth, is presented. It insists that a human being is
more than a statistical inference. The author argues that
"doing good" can be given content and substance and become an

overreaching goal for public personnel administration.

54. Cohen, Mark E.   "The 'Brave New Baby' and the Law:
    Fashioning Remedies for the Victims of In Vitro
    Fertilization." American Journal of Law and Medicine 4, 3
    (Fall 1978) 319-336.

The birth of the world's first "test-tube baby," a child
conceived by in vitro fertilization (IVF), raises serious
medical, ethical, and legal problems. The IVF process
includes fertilization of the oocytes, laparoscopy, and
embryo transplantation. There are serious risks of
birth-defective children born of this process. Arguments
favoring IVF use include: (1) the conceptus, not being
human, is not subject to moral consideration, and (2)
parental consent dissipates moral objections. Those against
IVF use argue that (A) the conceptus is life belonging to the
human species, (B) it is unethical to subject a conceptus to
unknown hazards, and (contingency coefficient) medical ethics
prescribing the safety of experimental subjects are violated.
While Department of Health, Education, and Welfare
regulations effectively control IVF activity, the Roe vs.
Wade decision supported the view that the state cannot
regulate IVF births. Government regulation of IVF should be
restricted to experimental guidelines. It would be
inappropriate to hold experimenters and parents liable for
the destruction of IVF conceptus unless the experimenter was
negligent in some way. Liability for the birth of a severely
defective IVF child may take three forms: (a) an action by
parents for wrongful birth, (b) an action for wrongful life,
or (c) an action for prenatal/preconception injury. Because
the IVF technique is dangerous, experimenters should be held
strictly liable for a defective child attributable to the IVF
technique. The legal system should not inhibit scientific
growth, but should protect human subjects who contribute to
that progress.

55. Conrad, Ann Patrick. "The Health Care Policy Pendulum: An
    Ethical Perspective." Social Thought 8, 1 (1982) 25-38.

Based on social work experience, the escalating interest
in ethical issues in the United States is noted. Although
scholarly literature is developing, particularly around
ethical dilemmas in direct practice, there is only beginning
utilization of value inclusive frameworks for analyzing
public policy. Recent shifts in health care policy are
analyzed for an ethical perspective utilizing an ethical
model for decision making based on the principles of

proportionalism. Health care legislation and its related
underlying philosophical rationale are conceptualized in
terms of discrete but overlapping phases. The expansion
phase, the period from the early 1960s through the mid-1970s,
was characterized by bills on community-based care,
prevention, training, and research, based on a philosophy
that persons are entitled to all that is necessary to promote
health. The period of cost containment, during the 1970s,
was characterized by frequency of regulatory and planning
activity, peer review, and increase of copayments for medical
care, and was accompanied by a more conservative
understanding of the obligation to insure the right to a
healthy existence. The current situation, with increasing
block grants, termed a period of delegation of
responsibility, is justified on the grounds of competition
and free enterprise, and results in a dilemma of entitlement
versus competition. The various value hierarchies
undergirding these two approaches were identified, the
importance placed by social work and other helping
professions on the common good is highlighted, drawbacks for
professionals and quality client service are discussed, and
the long and circuitous route to the common good when the
competition approach is taken is pointed out.

56. DeBakey, Michael E., and Lois DeBakey. "The Ethics and
    Economics of High-Technology Medicine." Comprehensive
    Therapy 9, 12 (December 1983) 6-16.

    Medicine has undergone major advances during recent
decades in the United States. These innovations have created
numerous ethical and social problems. Among them are
increasing costs, demographic changes, the growth of
high-technology medicine, governmental regulations, and
changing social values. Resolution of these controversies
requires realistic cost-benefit analyses. At the same time,
the United States medical system remains the best in the
world and has the capacity to solve these problems.

57. Denny, Brewster G. "Science and Public Policy." Public
    Administration Review 27 (June 1967) 95-133.

    Denny asserts in his introduction that "the impact of
science and technology in the contemporary world is so great
as to demand a fundamental examination of social
institutions, how they are changing" and their capacity to
incorporate examination of values in policy decisions. Denny
provides an introduction to a symposium on science and public
policy which raises many questions regarding the contemporary

impact of science and technology on the process of public administration. The author raises important questions regarding the ethical implication of the role of science in the practice of public policy and administration.

58. Flagg, Joan Margaret. Mental Health Policy and the Ideologies of Psychiatric and Mental Health Nurses. Ph.D. Dissertation, University of Texas at Austin (1984).

The purposes of the study were: (1) to describe the professional ideologies of specialists in psychiatric and mental health nursing as expressed through opinions and attitudes related to mental health policy alternatives; and (2) to describe the relationships between characteristics of the subjects and beliefs about mental health policy issues. Theoretical bases of the investigation were drawn from two major sources. Concepts from the sociology of knowledge were applied to understanding the development of professional ideologies through social process. Development of public policy was described through the application of systems theory. Psychiatric and mental health nursing was seen as developing to a significant degree out of government mental health policy and now concerned with providing input into further policy development.

Members of the American Nurses' Association Council of Specialists in Psychiatric and Mental Health Nursing (N = 403) completed a questionnaire developed for the study. The questionnaire consisted of 73 items to assess beliefs and opinions on mental health policy issues and questions related to respondent characteristics. Opinion items were factor-analyzed to identify belief patterns of the respondents. Four factors were identified and named according to their content: Mental Health Systems and Services; Locus of Responsibility; Medical Model Orientation; and Attitudes and Ethics. Respondents took a conservative position on expansion of publicly supported mental health care, but considered government responsible for providing services. Some aspects of a medical model approach to mental health were endorsed. Beliefs identified with community mental health ideology were supported.

Discriminant analyses were carried out with the opinion items as independent variables and demographic and professional characteristics of respondents as dependent variables. It was found that significant differences of opinion existed between subgroups on all the characteristics examined. In setting policy agendas and professional development goals, psychiatric and mental health nurses should be aware of both the shared core of beliefs and concerns and the significant differences of opinion on specific issues which exist within the discipline.

59. Forster, Jean L. "A Communitarian Ethical Model for Public Health Interventions: An Alternative to Individual Behavior Change Strategies." Journal of Public Health Policy 3, 2 (June 1982) 150-163.

Premature death, or death before age 65, is a serious problem in the United States, and is often caused by behavioral risk factors. The philosophy of policymakers is that since individual behavior causes health problems, individual change must constitute the solution. The fallacy of this argument is illustrated by citing statistics on the use of passive restraints as a preventive measure against traffic injuries. In spite of multimillion dollar efforts over a 20-year period to promote seat belt use, only 10% of automobile passengers use them. It is argued that communitarian tactics of coercion must replace the ethics of individual interest to achieve public health goals. Communitarian justifications for collective, coercive intervention based on the idea of the social values of a community are noted. 39 References. J. Cannon.

60. Gabor, Dennis. Inventing the Future. New York: Alfred Knopf (1964).

Gabor warns readers of the Age of Leisure in which new technological inventions and the work of a small minority is sufficient to keep the majority in idle luxury. His approach is to follow a piecemeal social engineering approach. He is concerned about trends towards self-destruction by war, over population, racial deterioration, and instability created by technology. He states that we cannot predict the future but that the future can be invented. Man's ability to invent has made human society what it is. This book analyzes some of the ethical questions associated with social and technological development.

61. Gershon, Eliot S. "Should Science Be Stopped: The Case of Recombinant DNA Research." Public Interest 71 (Spring 1983) 3-16.

This article raises concerns of those groups who wish to stop recombinant DNA research. It provides a case study of the political activities of a segment of the scientific

community. Gershon summarizes the events of 1974-75
moratoriums on DNA research. The author showed how
scientists and the scientific process responded to political
demands. The article illustrates how the bureaucratic
structure set up by the Federal government through NIH was
successful in developing scientific concensus in response to
new scientific findings.

62. Glazer, Myron. "Will Biology Transform the Humanities?" The
    Hastings Center Report 10, 6 (December 1980) 27-39.

This report includes three short articles which focus on
the pertinence of scientific theories and moral judgments.
The first article addresses the ethical implications of human
Sociobiology. Sociobiology is concerned with biology of
those groups and especially those aspects of demography,
genetic kinship, hierarchy, and communication that
constitutes qualities of a society.
    A second article addresses the question of natural
selection and human choice. The author states that natural
selection refers to the blind, automatic working out of
genotypic frequencies. The article raises the question,
"What are the appropriate ethical issues which best assure
the survival of genes like our own?"
    A third article focuses on "what is true and what is
possible for human beings from a biological perspective."
Humanists, as well as behaviorial and social scientists are
concerned about the definition of man as a unique human
being. The article addresses the ethical implications
associated with evolution of mankind.

63. Grad, Frank P. "Medical Ethics and the Law." The Annals of
    the American Academy of Political and Social Science 437
    (May 1978) 19-36.

Medicine, as a learned profession, has traditionally
insisted that the conduct of physicians be governed by its
own code of professional ethics. Increased government
regulation of the practice of medicine, however, has largely
substituted external, governmental regulation for earlier
ethical constraints. Government regulations have been
imposed both in response to greater risks in the practice of
medicine and in consequence of ever greater government
funding of health care. Though regulations reflect a
contemporary consensus on ethical attitudes, their
promulgation has narrowed the exercise of the physician's
independent ethical judgment. While the physician is
increasingly subject to legal requirements in his practice

and in such areas as informed consent, the use of human subjects in clinical research, genetic and biological research, and the management of the dying patient, his ethical sensitivity in complying with such requirements is still essential for the protection of patients.

64. Green, Harold P. "The Recombinant DNA Controversy: A Model of Public Influence." Bulletin of the Atomic Scientists 34, 9 (1978) 12-16.

This article examines recombinant DNA research for its ethical, scientific, and political aspects, focusing on the need for federal regulation and public policymaking. The time has arrived to address the public policy question of the interrelationships between science and public policy. The author draws comparisons between government regulatory controls on atomic energy and efforts to regulate recombinant DNA. Green makes a claim for limited restriction on scientists efforts to research DNA. He argues that in the arena of public policy decision-making, scientific truth will not prevail if it is handed down from on high.

65. Guttmacher, Sally. "Immigrant Workers: Health, Law, and Public Policy" Journal of Health Politics, Policy and Law 9, 3 (Fall 1984) 503-514.

Immigrant workers are a large segment of the lower echelon of the United States labor force; between 3.6 and 6 million of these workers and their families are living in the United States illegally. Following an examination of who the recent immigrants are, a discussion ensues on the ethical and policy issues surrounding their health needs and illegal status. Some implications of the Simpson-Mazzoli Immigrant and Reform Act, currently before Congress, are noted. It is concluded that: the illegal status of undocumented workers intensifies their health risks; the immigrants' responsibility for budget short-falls in public services is not as clearcut as frequently assumed; and legislation aimed at regulating the status of immigrant workers in the United States is unlikely to solve many of the central problems.

66. Handler, Philip. "Public Doubts About Science." Science 208, 4448 (June 6 1980) 1093.

Public doubt has emerged both about science and about the progress of the human race. This has brought about the emergence of antiscience attitudes, which should be opposed strongly. The involvement of scientists in public policy has helped to encourage this attitude through confusion of scientific and political/ideological concerns. Scientists can best serve society by adherence to the ethics of science, open admission of ignorance or uncertainty on certain questions, and clear advocacy of the value of science.

67. Hayzelden, J. E. "The Value of Human Life." Public Administration 46 (Winter 1968) 427-441.

The objective of this article is to show that a figure for the value of human life is often required in cost-benefit studies and to outline some of the ways in which a calculation may be made. The author argues that acceptance of cost-benefit analysis as a decision-making strategy suggests that we calculate the worth of human beings to society. The author raises numerous moral and ethical questions associated with this policy question and applies his model to the British system.

68. Hsiao, William Ching Lung. Market Structure and Physician Fees. Ph.D. Dissertation, Harvard University (1982).

The market for physician services is complicated by four factors: uncertainty, asymmetrical information, agency and third party payment of fees. These factors create market distortions including moral hazard, professional autonomy and dominance, and regulations. Moreover, the price and quantity of physician services are not determined by a single market, but by the joint action of insurance and physician markets. The allocative efficiency of medical care, therefore, hinges on a set of complex interactions among patients, doctors, and insurers.

This thesis tries to achieve four major goals: (1) expand the available analytical information of the health insurance market; (2) examine the market structure of the physician services and the market power of physicians over price and quantity decisions; (3) analyze the relationship and interaction between physician and insurance markets; (4) examine several hypotheses regarding physician fee-setting behavior.

69. Knowles, John H. "Introduction (To an Issue on Health Care)." Daedalus 106(1) (1977) 1-7.

Discusses health care costs, quality, and accessibility. Health care is a private, pluralistic, acute, curative system favoring the elderly. Health insurance has emphasized

hospital and surgical expenses. There has been increasing
specialization in medical education. Public health interests
are ignored by medical education and practice. Government
support for public health is leveling off. Medical ethics
and training are receiving new emphasis. Interest in
national health insurance remains high. Despite advances,
many Americans suffer intolerable levels of deprivation and
ill health.

70. Lake, Randall Alan. The Ethics of Rhetoric and the Rhetoric
    of Ethics in the Abortion Controversy. Ph.D.
    Dissertation, University of Kansas (1982).

    The abortion controversy represents one of the most hotly
    contested, and seemingly intractable, issues confronting
    public policy-makers. Both anti-abortionists and repealists
    employ a variety of value-based arguments in attempts to
    promulgate their views.

    This study examines the relationships between the fields
    of ethics and argumentation as these relationships are
    manifested in the abortion dispute. Chapter 1 explicates the
    traditional view of the ethics of argument. Chapter 2
    identifies and illustrates the essential arguments advanced
    by both anti-abortionists and repealists. Chapter 3 analyzes
    the divergent "moral points of view" implicit within these
    arguments in three areas: the nature of morality; the moral
    character of humans; and the nature of persuasion in the
    moral arena. Chapter 4 argues that the persuasive power of
    abortion rhetoric derives from its exploitation of the
    hortatory negative as a linguistic resource. Chapter 5
    reconsiders the relationship between ethics and argument,
    emphasizing the role of rational consistency as an ethical
    yardstick.

    The study is based principally on the transcripts of
    Congressional hearings on abortion. Other primary source
    materials include various books, journals, periodicals, and
    newspapers in the fields of rhetorical theory, ethics,
    argumentation, and the abortion question.

71. La Porte, Todd A. "Politics and 'Inventing the Future':
    Perspectives in Science and Government." Public
    Administration Review (June 1967) 117.

    Recent developments in the tone and character of public
    affairs have been increasingly influenced by the growing
    interdependence of science, technology, and the Federal

government. The net effect of this interdependence is an
expanding capacity of our government to "invent the future."
This paper attempts to frame a perspective for study to
stimulate new information and new alternatives for public
policy. La Porte asks, "What is possible in the political
and social evolution of man?" Whether explicitly or not, the
question is now being answered. The future holds enormous
danger. This is a significant policy issue that needs debate
and definition.

72. Markey, Kathleen. "Federal Regulation of Fetal Research:
    Toward a Public Policy Founded on Ethical Reasoning."
    University Miami Law Review 31, 3 (Spring 1977) 675-696.

The 1975 federal regulations on fetal research reflect the
recommendations of a national study commission that
formulated a policy based upon broad ethical considerations.
The fetus is now accorded comprehensive protection in medical
experimentation-protection so comprehensive that necessary
and valuable benefits to future fetuses must be given up.
The legal and ethical rights of the fetus are described and
the history and present status of the regulation of fetal
research explored. It is suggested that the regulations be
carefully modified to permit greater latitude in conducting
research on drug pharmacology in aborted fetuses. Potential
benefit of research directed toward understanding the facts
that modify placental transfer of drugs and their subsequent
movement into the fetus has been given up for a small amount
of protection. This type of research should be conducted
within carefully constructed guidelines on fetuses about to
be aborted.

73. McCormick, Richard A. "Bioethics in the Public Form."
    Health and Society 61, 1 (Winter 1983) 113-126.

Public policy is, and ought to be, concerned with the
welfare of human beings across a broad spectrum of
circumstances and conditions. This subject is explored from
the perspective of a Catholic moral theologian serving as a
public policy consultant on in vitro fertilization to the
Ethics Advisory Board. Evaluative judgments made by the
Board are not edicts; they leave matters open for
reconsideration and revision, while providing a basis for
policy decisions for the present.

74. Mechanic, David. "Ethics, Justice, and Medical Care
    Systems." The Annals of the American Academy of Political
    and Social Science 437 (May 1978) 74-85.

As medical costs mount and government pays more, explicit forms of medical care rationing are likely to come. Rationing may be imposed through financial barriers for the patient in the form of coinsurance and deductibles or in limitations on the funds, facilities, and services available. Imposing barriers to access on the theory that consumers are in a good position to make necessary differentiations places the burden of rationing on the patient who is least able to make the decision rationally, and places the poor, who have the least medical knowledge, in particular jeopardy. Other alternatives include the introduction of fixed budgets requiring professionals to establish priorities or administrative decisions that prescribe the facilities and services available to various populations. Existing research indicates that the consequences of some rationing approaches are inconsistent with theoretical assumptions. The means developed for rationing must encompass equity, as well as efficiency, and produce care that is dignified.

75. Mesthene, Emmanuel G. "The Impact of Science on Public Policy." _Public Administration Review._ (June 1967) 97.

Our newfound ability to change the physical world with science requires the creation and administration of sound policy. The author argues that the single most pervasive impact of science and technology on politics is the shortening of the time span of physical change to the same order as that of social and political actions.

76. Miller, Paula Jean, Alice M. Rivlin, and P. Michael Timpane (eds). "Ethical and Legal Issues of Social Experimentation." _Political Science Quarterly_ 91, 3 (Fall, 1976) 536-537.

The decrease in new funding available for social programs has resulted in calls for demonstrating the cost-effectiveness of publicly funded programs. This has resulted in the use of experimental programs to demonstrate their effectiveness before moving to large scale implementation. The trend towards these pilot projects, along with publicized unethical research, has resulted in a debate about the ethics of social experimentation. The reviewed volume includes discussion of 14 areas in this debate.

77. Norman, Jane C. "Medical Ethics and the Law, Implications for Public Policy." _Legal Aspects of Medical Practice_ 11

(April 1983) 5-6.

Norman asserts that this volume addresses the toughest issues in medical ethics today. In addition to chapters concerning abortion, informed consent, genetic engineering, and other "obligatory" topics, this book treats issues of social justice in the health care planning and the values promoted by federal health policies. Norman considers the book must reading for health planners and legislators.

78. Reagan, Michael D. "R and D: Suggestions for an Allocations Framework." Public Administration Review (June 1967) 104.

Policy for science is not a problem in the natural sciences, but a social or social science problem. This paper provides fresh ideas by suggesting an approach to research and development appropriations. The author states that the overall case for Federal support must rest on social benefit. In this article he spells out a rationale for research support. He concludes stating that a successful funding program will require far more through understanding than we now possess of the relationship between science-using and science-generating activities.

79. Reiser, Stanley Joel. "Human Experimentation and the Convergence of Medical Research and Patient Care." The Annals of the American Academy of Political and Social Science 437 (May 1978) 8-18.

This article discusses the growth of experimentation on human subjects in the United States and Great Britain in the twentieth century. It focuses on the linkage that developed in medicine between research and patient care. The circumstances that helped to forge this linkage are described as: (1) a notion that the uncertainty of outcome common to activities in medical research and practice basically joins the two; (2) a concept of medical education that research training creates analytic skills essential in providing good patient care; (3) governmental policies which fiscally link medical research to medical education; and (4) the view that patient care and research can be simultaneously and ethically pursued by a given physician on a given patient. In the 1950s warnings were heard that the zeal for medical knowledge could lead a scientist whose technical background might overshadow his sense of clinical responsibility, to disregard the well-being of his research subject. These policies must be reappraised if an equitable balance is to exist between the goal of gaining knowledge through research and care for patients through practice.

80. Rhoads, Steven E. "How Much Should We Spend to Save a Life?"
    Public Interest 51 (Spring 1978) 74-92.

    The article analyzes various approaches of economists as
    to the need for calculating a value for life. The discussion
    focuses on the advocates of two general approaches: 1) The
    "discounted future earnings" and the "willingness-to-pay"
    methodology. Alternatives to the WTP methodology involve two
    studies examining job market decisions, specifically
    work-related risk. Factors involved in deciding who should
    receive lifesaving therapy and the equalizing of lifesaving
    expenditures are discussed. In conclusion, public policy on
    lifesaving programs will not achieve completely satisfactory
    solutions but, if research is to be successful, the cost of
    delivering therapeutic services should also be considered.

81. Rose-Ackerman, Susan. "Mental Retardation and Society: The
    Ethics and Politics of Normalization." Ethics 93, 1 (Oct
    1982) 81-101.

    A survey of the philosophical and political issues
    underlying recent attempts to deinstitutionalize the mentally
    retarded. How several general normative political theories
    would deal with the mentally retarded is examined. While
    some common normative positions are incoherent when applied
    to mental retardation, other theories are shown to generate
    internally consistent views. The relationship between these
    theories and the positions of advocates for the retarded is
    discussed, and how principles conflict with each other under
    plausible interpretations of the facts is illustrated. The
    links between private interests and philosophical principles
    are explored, and an analysis offered of why some past
    alliances are breaking up, and the way in which advocates of
    normalization have been forced to compromise their principles
    to obtain public funds for the retarded.

82. Stein, Jane. "Questions of Life and Death Weighed by Medical
    Ethics Watchdog Commission." National Journal 14
    (December 11, 1982) 2119-2121.

    The report of a presidential commission on ethical
    problems in medicine and medical research could shape
    government policies on the way health care is delivered
    (impact of the President's Commission for the Study of
    Ethical Problems in Medicine and Biomedical and Behavioral
    Research).

The outstanding questions are how much health care can society afford? Does society have an ethical obligation to ensure equitable access to health care for all? And are there ethical ways to cut medical cost? This commission was charged with reviewing issues of medical research. The article is a review of their work and report on their findings.

83. Stephens, Jerome. "Biomedical Research and the Need for a Public Policy." Policy Studies Journal 1, 3 (1973) 183-186.

Urges legal regulation of experimentation on humans. This article addresses the lack of protection for individuals who are, willingly or unwillingly, subjects of biomedical experimentation. He contends that there is a lack of adequate protection in law, national health agencies, ethical codes, and institutional review committees. Stephens argues that there is now no public policy that adequately protects the individual from experimentation. He states that the last time a comprehensive act regulating human experimentation was offered in the U.S. was 1900.

84. Stover, Carl F. "Industry, Technology, and Metropolitan Problem." Public Administration Review (June 1967) 1107.

Technology, its application and power in communities has an ethical diversion. This article alerts the reader to be more cognizance of the effects of possible technological commitments on a community. Industry must be embraced carefully to avoid the improper delegation of public authority to private hands and ensure the dominance of public goals. He argues that technology and the ability to use it are forms of power, and as in all cases of power, must be held responsible.

85. Toner, James H. "Sisyphus as a Soldier: Ethics, Exigencies, and the American Military." Parameters 7, 4 (1977) 2-12.

The author's objective is to discuss, in ethical terms, the major issues and tensions which are produced when the freedoms of a democratic society interact with the requirements of the military and of national defense. The author notes two general types of recent criticisms directed at the military, one by revisionist historians who impute blame for international tensions and aggression to the United States military, and the other by critics of the

military-industrial establishment. Noting that these are
criticisms of the military's situation, not of the military
itself, the author points out that military reforms, as
exemplified by changes in the Uniform Code of Military
Justice, have centered on the ethical questions of the rights
of soldiers. These involve resolution of the basic dilemma
of at what points liberties of citizens infringe on a
soldier's duty. Concluding with a discussion of national
defense policy couched in similar terms, the author argues
that the central question is a macro-level reformulation of
the earlier problem: how to judge which means are
appropriate for use in defending a democratic society. For
both cases, conscience must set the limits of action.

86. Waltz, Jon R., and Carol R. Thigpen. "Genetic Screening and
     Counseling: The Legal and Ethical Issues." Northwestern
     University Law Review 68, 4 (September-October 1973)
     696-768.

     The era of biological engineering, the process of
manipulating genes, is now upon us. Possible programs range
from voluntary genetic screening for defective babies to
compulsory eugenics to breed superior human qualities.
Federal and state laws have been passed relating to
large-scale genetic screening, notably the May 1972 National
Sickle Cell Anemia Control Act. Requiring an individual to
submit to a screening blood test is a considerable invasion
of personal privacy. The Supreme Court has been reluctant to
uphold any laws significantly interfering with the marriage
relationship; however, the eradication of certain genetic
diseases can be accomplished only through prohibition of
reproduction by designated couples. Basic justifications for
compulsory controls have been: (1) the safeguarding of the
public health and welfare; (2) the proper allocation of
economic resources; and (3) the reduction of human suffering.
At this point voluntary genetic screening procedures should
be made readily available which also include confidentiality,
community representation, and counseling. Legal issues
relating to genetic counseling include: (A) faulty
counseling based on a mistaken diagnosis; (B) failure to
inform the parents of a probably defective baby; and (C)
(contingency coefficient) "wrongful life" suits brought by
defective children not prenatally diagnosed.

87. "Ethics and Government (Emergence of a Worldwide Environment
     Ethic and its Impact in Such Areas as Energy, the Economy
     and Human Health; Special Issue)." EPA (Environmental
     Protection Agency) Journal 5 (November-December 1979)

2-35.

88. "President's Commission for the Study of Ethical Problems in
     Medicine and Biomedical and Behavioral Research." (1982).

Chapter V

Ethics and the Interrelationship of
Government and Business

89. Belt, Beverly Lynn. "Conflict of Interests Involving Private Practitioners Representing Cities and Counties." Journal of Legal Profession 6 (1981) 251-261.

What is the ethical responsibility of a lawyer who represents conflicting interests, when on behalf of one client, it is his duty to contend for that which duty to another requires him to oppose. This problem is particularly prevalent in situations involving present or former city and county attorneys. The author makes specific guidelines for attorneys in communities where a conflict may present problems.

90. Bowman, James S. "Managerial Ethics in Business and Government." Business Horizons 19 (October 1976) 48-54.

A new skepticism of business and government in the public's mind has played upon a deepened traditional suspicion of large organizations. The data presented in this article reveal that business and government executives are interested in these concerns. This article discusses the findings of two research surveys to compare the views of business managers to those of public managers.

91. Clark, Wesley C. "Public Administration and Private Interest." Annals of the American Academy of Political and Social Science 280 (March 1952) 67-76.

Though pessimistic in viewing the possibilities for high moral standards in government service, Clark cites such factors as "moral tone of the nation," procedures, staff, leadership, and public communication as keys to making sound administrative decisions.

92. Clinard, Marshall B. Corporate Ethics and Crime: The Role of Middle Management. Beverly Hills: Sage Publications (1983).

This book presents views about middle management's opinions regarding corporate ethical, unethical, or illegal behavior. What middle management has to say about those matters should increase our understanding of the processes within large corporations that account for them. This manuscript includes lengthy interviews with retired Fortune 500 middle management executives. Issues addressed include why some corporations are more ethical than others, the extent to which top management sets the policies that lead either to ethical or unethical behavior, the ethical culture

in organizations and whether industry self-regulation would
be superior to government regulations.

93. DeGregori, Thomas R. "Ethics and Economic Inquiry: The
     Ayres-Knight Debate and the Problem of Economic Order."
     American Journal of Economics and Sociology 36, 1
     (January 1977) 41-50.

     The author examines the debate between Clarence E. Ayres
     and Frank H. Knight, which appeared in the "International
     Journal of Ethics," 1934-1936, in order to explore some of
     the basic philosophical issues of economics. Also, it is
     believed that this debate has potential for helping to
     understand current problems. Ayres found the central issue
     of economic inquiry to be the problem of economic order and
     the legitimacy of government economic intervention. Knight,
     on the other hand, denies any normative implications to the
     economists' concept of order. Thus, there is one side of
     economics that Knight would call mechanical or scientific
     and that Ayres would argue is normative. Policy
     implications of this are briefly discussed. While Ayres
     argues that neo-classical economics contain value-laden
     propositions while claiming to be ethically neutral, Knight
     defends these propositions as being value-free. It is
     explained that an obstacle preventing economics from fully
     becoming a science is that it deals with actions toward ends
     that cannot fully be known in advance. The author states
     that Knight's conclusions are very close to the modern
     theories of constitutional change of Buchanan and Tullock:
     a theory of status quo and not of social change. Ayres more
     appropriately addressed the question of a theory of social
     change and the construction of a new economic order. The
     key historical question to Ayres was the source of economic
     progress: industrial efficiency. Concluding, the two are
     compared as follows: 1) Knight seeks to have people be
     moral and change themselves and then by mutual understanding
     change the world; 2) Ayres seeks to have us look beyond
     ourselves to the truth implicit in what we have created.

94. Engelhardt, Joseph Louis. Normative and Descriptive Ethics
     in the Insurance Industry: Views of Insurance
     Professionals. Ph.D. Dissertation, University of Georgia
     (1984).

     A self-administered survey questionnaire was mailed to a
     random sample (N=1,500) of insurance professionals. The
     sample of two subgroups: agents (N=900) and executives
     (N=600). All respondents received the same questionnaire

which consisted of twenty-five neutral statements. Each respondent was asked to view each statement from his or her opinion of the current state of ethics within the insurance industry (descriptive ethics) and of what each thought that state of ethics should be (normative ethics). Also, each respondent was asked to give his or her definition of "insurance ethics," how each thought those ethics could be improved, and, finally, certain classification or demographic data.

The descriptive responses to the neutral statements pointed to the following conclusions: (1) insurance professionals indicated a genuine, down-to-earth view both of the consumers' rights and of their business needs; (2) though significant differences were found between the sample subgroup, these differences were not substantive, but rather differences of degree only; (3) the consuming public's opinion of the insurance industry may have over-sensitized some respondents, possibly causing them to view neutral statements personally; (4) insurance professionals seem to have a fairly broad view of the state of insurance ethics within the industry as a whole, not just within the respondents' own particular segments.

The normative responses to the neutral statements pointed to the following conclusions: (1) insurance professionals indicated a genuine, down-to-earth view both of the consumers' rights and of their business needs; (2) significant differences were not substantive, but rather a matter of degree only; (3) normative responses indicated a stronger ethical bent, though it may not have.

95. Hill, Peter J. "Ethics and the Marketplace." Cato Journal 2, 1 (1982) 165-204.

Advances the theory, from an ethical perspective, that there is little public interest in achieving efficiency in water pollution policy. Hill presents a strong argument for extending the use of private property and the market forces where possible. He addresses some of the common ethical objectives to private property and market opinions. The general thrust of the article is to support market competition values in relation to business ethics.

96. Leys, Wayne A. R. "Ethics in American Business and Government: The Confused Issues." The Annals of the American Academy of Political and Social Science 378 (July 1968) 34-44.

"A comparison of American executives with their
predecessors of a century ago reveals a heightening of moral
awareness and concern. In both business and government,
more duties are recognized today than was the case in the
nineteenth century. There is also concern for a greater
range of values. But this sort of responsibility is
dismissed as unimportant by some critics who claim that the
managerial class is failing to come to grips with the
international and interracial conflicts of our time. It
cannot be denied that some worldshaking decisions have been
made recklessly. Although it is difficult to identify the
'great decisions,' some industrialists and some politicians
seem to recognize that they have an obligation, and stand
ready to negotiate some new policies. The peculiar
difficulty of the present crisis is that preindustrial
populations, both here and abroad, cannot formulate
actionable demands of the kind that corporations and
existing agencies of government can satisfy. We should at
least consider the alternative of protected preindustrial
islands in our automated sea, where unskilled labor might
earn a living with self-respect.

97. Majerus, Raymond. "Nowhere To Go But Up: Corporation
    Ethics in the U.S. Economy." Review of Social Economy
    40, 3 (1982) 407-416.

This paper explores two themes. First, that the
overriding economic and political power of giant
corporations requires a governmental role centered on
protecting the public from the actions and decisions of
entities that exist only to make a profit. Second, that
such a government role must be supplemented with a strong
labor movement dedicated to serving workers who would
otherwise be reduced to cogs in a machine. He contends
that a return to ethical values in looking at the economy
could not be more important. He concludes by stating that a
society that seeks to meet standards based on ethical
principles cannot exempt its economy and industry from those
ethics.

98. McKean, Roland N. "Some Economic Aspects of
    Ethical-Behavioral Codes." Political Studies 27, 2 (June
    1979) 251-265.

Some informal rules merely save decision-making costs in
social exchanges, but we try to use others as social
contracts to produce public goods. (In fact, effective

ethical-behavioral constraints may be essential to retention and useful functioning of markets and democratic government.) Ethical-behavioral tenets are themselves public goods; however, adherence to them is vulnerable to cheap- or free-rider difficulties. In the long run, therefore, desirable informal laws will be underprovided. Nonetheless, according to both theory and observation, individuals sometimes overturn their free-riderism, compulsively sacrifice their selfish interests, and maintain useful customs and rules. Conditions that determine the costs and "indoctrinated" or psychic rewards to individuals for their adherence are discussed. These conditions will shape the degree of underproduction of advantageous behavioral codes.

99. Miller, Gifford Willis. The Ethical Conduct and Behavior of Public Executives Compared to that of Corporate Executives. Ph.D. Dissertation, Claremont Graduate School (1981).

The purpose of this study was to compare ethical standards and preferred conduct between top executives in the public sector and top executives in the private sector to determine if there was any difference.

On the basis of an analysis of both research literature and the relative position of public and private sector executives two hypotheses were developed. Executives in the private sector were expected to view ethical conduct and concepts as being of less importance to organizational goals than do executives in the public sector. Second, public executives were expected to conduct their professional affairs, i.e., take actions, in accordance with a higher level of ethical standards than do private sector executives.

A comparison of the two groups indicated the level of ethics to be relatively high, at least no unethical practices were revealed. Further, there was no statistically significant differences between the two groups for either hypothesis. The results were interpreted as showing that public and private sector executives have substantial similarities in apparent ethical views.

100. Sonnenfeld, Jeffrey Alan. Corporate Views of the Public Interest: Perceptions of the Forest Products Industry. D.B.A. Dissertation, Harvard University (1981).

This research studied the public affairs information
gathering and responsiveness of seven of the largest U.S.
forest products companies. Over the last two decades, the
managerial significance of issues in the public affairs
sector of the business environment has, in many ways,
matched the significance of issues in the market and
technological sectors of this environment. The specific
purpose of the present research was to better understand the
internal company preparedness for a very complex public
affairs environment. The central focus was on the
relationship of a company's structure to its responsiveness
to public affairs.

The conceptual model guiding this research suggested that
the public affairs responsiveness of large corporations can
be understood through a metaphorical parallel in the human
sensory mechanism.

The findings confirmed the existence of strong
differences in perceptions or biases by company departments.
Furthermore, these departments acquired information in very
different ways and relied on very different sources. This
study also detected substantial company by company
differences in both the sensitivity of corporate structure
and the sensitivity of corporate culture to the public
affairs issues. The sensitivity of overall corporate
structure seemed to contribute to a company's responsiveness
or alertness to public affairs. A company's cultural
sensitivity, however, seemed to affect its social
responsibility, or ethics in public affairs performance.

101. Vogel, David. "The Responsibilities of Multinational
     Corporations." Society 16, 3, 119 (March-April 1979)
     52-56.

A useful way of acquiring some perspective on the ethical
dilemmas associated with international corporate conduct is
to place some contemporary issues in a broader context.
Examined are four sets of issues: the impact of economic
growth on peace and justice, the implications of an
investment in repressive nations, corporate social
responsibility abroad, and overseas payments. In the final
analysis, it is the nation-state that will determine the
conduct of the multinational corporation; governments remain
the world's most important actors. Yet the role of the
multinational corporation remains far from a passive one.
Those who make decisions for global enterprises need to be
encouraged, pressured, and even inspired to make decisions

that show as much sensitivity as possible to human rights, social justice, and world peace.

102. Waldenstrom, Erland. "Corruption in Business: A Common Problem for Governments and Enterprises." Skandinaviska Enskilda Banken Quarterly Review (1978) 25-29.

This article relates attempts by the International Chamber of Commerce (ICC) to investigate the occurrence of corruption in the business world and to propose measures for combating it. The paper focuses on developing countries of the USA, France, Germany, Belgium and Japan. The ICC proposals call on businesses to work with governments to establish acceptable ethical guidelines for international business.

103. Witherspoon, Ruth Aurora. "Multinational Corporations – Governmental Regulation of Business Ethics Under the Foreign Corrupt Practices Act of 1977: An Analysis." Dickerson Law Review 87 (Spring 1983) 531-593.

This article focuses on the Foreign Corrupt Practices Act of 1977 by looking first hand at the background against which it was enacted and its history and development. The article discusses Act operation and implementation and assesses the validity of criticism directed at the Act and proposed solutions addressing those criticisms. The Act has raised a number of concerns and some problems, not only for those required to comply with the Act, but for those who must enforce it as well.

Chapter VI

Codes of Ethics for Policy Analysis

104. Allen, William H. "The 'Revolving Door' - Should It Be
      Stopped?" (A.B.A. National Conference on Federal
      Regulation) Administrative Law Review 32 (Spring 1980)
      383-409.

      Legal entrapment has been justified as a defense in
      government official bribery cases and other
      confrontationless crimes. The two prevailing views on what
      constitutes entrapment in the American legal system are: 1)
      The subjective theory, which permits entrapment only when
      the government trick gives the defendant the criminal
      design; and 2) The objective theory, which places the focus
      upon the government's actions, rather than upon the
      defendant's mental state. The Supreme Court has favored the
      subjective interpretation. Ambiguities and unclear legal
      and moral issues are examined. A distinction must first be
      made between the disposition to crime, which cannot be
      implanted, and the intention to commit a specific crime
      which can be implanted. Confusion also surrounds the notion
      of culpability of a defendant lured into crime. It is
      argued that the average-man standard is better than the
      predisposition standard because: 1) It limits what the
      government may do, regardless of the dispositions of any
      defendant; and 2) It avoids discrimination against those
      whose prior criminal records would be considered evidence of
      a disposition to crime.

105. Altman, Andrew, and Steven Lee. "Legal Entrapment."
      Philosophy and Public Affairs 12, 1 (Winter 1983) 51-69.

      In our legal system entrapment is sometimes allowed as a
      defense in cases where agents of the government have been
      involved in the commission of the crime with which the
      defendant is charged. Whether one regards it as a
      legitimate defense depends to a large degree upon what type
      of state conduct is considered to constitute entrapment.
      However, the courts and legal commentators have not spoken
      with a single voice in articulating a rationale for the idea
      that there are some types of state involvement in crime that
      should be regarded as sufficient grounds for acquitting a
      defendant who has been the target of such involvement. This
      article examines these issues and how they might be
      resolved.

106. Amy, Douglas J. "Why Policy Analysis and Ethics Are
      Incompatible." Journal of Policy Analysis and Management
      3, 4 (Summer 1984) 573-591.

Commentators in the field of policy analysis have argued
persuasively for the inclusion of ethical evaluations in the
analytic process; yet most practitioners in the policy field
avoid analyzing moral issues. Standard explanations for
this neglect of ethics tend to be inadequate; furthermore,
assertions that normative analysis is unnecessary,
impractical, impossible, or undesirable are demonstrably
weak. Political factors, on the other hand, provide a
clearer understanding of the neglect of ethics. Ethical
inquiry is shunned because it frequently threatens the
professional and political interests of both analysts and
policymakers. The administrator, legislator, bureaucracy,
and profession of policy analysis itself all resist the
potential challenges of moral evaluation.

107. Armstrong, DeWitt C., III, and George A. Graham. "Ethical
      Preparation for the Public Service." The Bureaucrat 4
      (April 1975) 5-22.

Despite such problems as shifting public opinion, early
socialization of individuals to varying ethical codes, and
the laxness of standards by public officials, the authors
argue that professional education can play a large role in
expanding the individual's analytical and perceptual skills
regarding ethical conflicts and values through use of the
case study approach both in undergraduate courses and in
graduate schools.

108. Austin, David M. "Administrative Practice in Human
      Services: Future Directions for Curriculum Development."
      The Journal of Applied Behavioral Science 19, 2 (May
      1983) 141-152.

The practice of administration in human services programs
has distinctive characteristics that distinguish it from
business and public administration. A specialized
curriculum that tries to integrate administrative features
and the political economy and other elements of human
services administration is needed. Some key aspects of the
macropolitical, operational-political, and
interorganizational-political economies are identified. In
comments on "Administrative Practice in Human Services:
Future Directions for Curriculum Development," Jack
McDonough (University of California, Los Angeles) contrasts
the emphasis on integrative skills in graduate social work
education and graduate business programs. Recommendations
for adapting certain competitive business techniques for
"pluralistic environments" to human services administration

are offered. In additional comments on "Administrative
Practice in Human Services: Future Directions for
Curriculum Development," Edward J. Mullen (University of
Chicago, IL) focuses on the normative character of
administration in social services provision. Donald C.
King and Mary E. Correa (Purdue University, West Lafayette,
IN) declare that David M. Austin has not adequately reckoned
with the extensive range of agencies that are included in
the designation "human service agencies." Like the
difference between nonprofit hospitals and those run for
profit, agency types are important. In reply to Professor
McDonough, Mullen, King, and Correa, David M. Austin
summarizes comments, and addresses aspects of ethics and
performance of human service agencies in relation to
profit/nonprofit perspectives and management systems.

109. Bailey, Stephen K. "Ethics and the Public Service." Public
     Administration Review 24 (December 1964) 234-243.

Now a seminal essay on the fundamental importance of the
individual in establishing ethics within the public service,
Bailey calls for "mental attitudes" demonstrating an
understanding of the complexities of government and "moral
qualities" demonstrating an ability to operationalize moral
concepts in the face of complexity. The blend is needed
because "virtue without understanding can be quite as
disastrous as understanding without virtue."

Building upon the "uncommon wisdom" and personal example
of the late Paul H. Appleby, Dean of the Maxwell School,
Syracuse University, and elaborating on some of the
fragments which Dean Appleby scattered throughout his
writings and teachings, the author examines the mental
attitudes and moral qualities necessary to an explicit
theory of personal ethics in the public service. "The three
essential mental attitudes are: (1) A recognition of the
moral ambiguity of all men and of all public policies; (2)
A recognition of the contextual forces which condition moral
priorities in the public service; and (3) A recognition of
the paradoxes of procedures. The essential moral qualities
of the ethical public servant are: (1) optimism; (2)
courage; and (3) fairness tempered by charity."

110. Baker, C. A. "Ethics in the Public Service." Journal of
     Administration Overseas 10 (January 1971) 22-32.

Baker calls on "public servants" to think of themselves and make decisions as if they were "trustees" for the public in carrying out their responsibilities, thus building up the reserve of respect so important in running the government.

111. Banfield, Edward C. "Corruption as a Feature of Governmental Organization." Journal of Law and Economics 18 (December 1975) 587-605.

Banfield identifies seven features of government which contribute to dilemmas for employees: fragmentation of authority; reduced role of money as a motivator for performance; fragmented legal controls; barriers to firing employees; prevalence of "informal deals"; concern with impact of election results; and lack of competition. Chances for internal controls seem slim since he contends that "presumably the culture that is being formed today contains a much smaller stock of dependability than did that formed a generation or two or three ago."

112. Benveniste, Guy. "On a Code of Ethics for Policy Experts." Journal of Policy Analysis and Management 3, 4 (Summer 1984) 561-572.

Advances in science and technology have exposed society to risks of unprecedented magnitude, which sometimes must be faced on very short notice, as in the field of nuclear power. Those developments have greatly increased the significance of the opinions of policy experts. When adversaries are pitted against one another on such issues, the risk that policy experts may lose legitimacy in the eyes of the public is very high. At such times, the concern grows that the experts' views may be influenced by pressure from their principals or by conflicts of personal interest. One step that could reduce the risk of a loss of legitimacy for policy experts is to develop a code of ethics, which would include such issues as: defining the responsibility of the expert, identifying unacceptable conflicts of interest, determining the expert's obligations regarding secrecy and disclosure, and developing standards for the process of decision making in emergencies.

113. Blake, Eugene Carson. "Should the Code of Ethics in Public Life be Absolute or Relative?" Annals of the American Academy of Political and Social Science 363 (January 1966) 4-11.

This well-known American religious leader explains that

the paradox of absolutism and relativism as solutions to ethical dilemmas can best be met by blending the two into "contextual ethics" in which the reality of the decision context is acknowledged.

114. Bok, Derek. "Can Ethics Be Taught?" Change 8, 9 (October 1976) 26-30.

Bok calls for moral education in colleges and universities using the "applied ethics" approach. While acknowledging that this may not make students more moral, Bok believes it may encourage students to define more carefully what they do believe.

115. Bowman, James S. "Cheating in the Classroom." News for Teachers of Political Science. 29 Spring 1981.

This article deals with one of the most difficult issues in higher education: cheating. The author outlines the problems associated with academic dishonesty. He discusses the seriousness of the problem and reviews the literature in this area. Bowman then demonstrates how a faculty member can encourage academic honesty.

116. Bowman, James S. "The Management of Ethics: Codes of Conduct in Organizations." Public Personnel Management 10, 1 (1981) 59-66.

This article discusses the role of the individual and the organization in the management of ethics. A device, a working social principle to implement ethics in administration is analyzed by reporting the attitudes and actions of managers in government and business.

117. Bowman, James S., editor. Essentials of Management: Ethical Values, Attitudes, and Action. National University Publications, Associated Faculty Press. Port Washington, NY 1983.

Since administrators face complicated ethical issues in organizations and in society, they are finding it increasingly necessary to expand their knowledge about managerial ethics. An executive today, in fact, can hardly afford not to study the subject. There is, however, a general lack of teaching and training materials in this field. Specifically, there are few that address these questions in the public and private sectors of the economy as they affect the administrator.

This collection aims at enlarging the administrator's understanding of the nature of ethics involved in his daily work by offering analytical studies of, and meaningful guidelines for, managerial situations. If the study of ethical puzzles in organizations is to be fruitful, in other words, then it must concentrate on problems central to management.

This book provides materials to assist managers and future managers to develop and/or maintain, personal and organizational codes of honorable performance.

The focus is on the middle manager and organizational problems of immediate significance to students of administration in the classroom or office. Both the future executive and today's executive, as decision-makers, must choose among values in making policies. Therefore, the issues here are examined from a manager's point of view; values of employees and their organizations are explored, and actions that individuals and institutions can take are discussed.

118. Buchanan, James M. "Ethical Rules, Expected Values and Large Numbers." Ethics 76, 1 (October 1965) 1-13.

A paper "concerned exclusively with an individual's choice among ethical rules and with the possibilities of predicting this choice." The author believes that we need to examine "the tradeoffs between voluntarist ethics and legislated morals."

119. Caiden, Gerald E., and Naomi J. Caiden. "Administrative Corruption." Public Administration Review 37, 3 (May-June 1977) 301-309.

Arguing that studying corruption as a structural system problem for government will be more productive than treating it as an individual, moral issue, the authors offer a number of hypotheses to "form the starting point for serious research into administrative corruption."

120. Callender, Clarence N., and James C. Charlesworth, Special Editors. "Ethical Standards in American Public Life." Annals of the American Academy of Political and Social Science 280 (March 1952).

Includes 19 articles on standards of ethics, public

morality, election and government agencies, sources of
ethical dilemmas and how to measure ethical standards;
articles indexed separately.

121. Carrol, James D. "Education for the Public Trust: Learning
      to Live With the Absurd." The Bureaucrat 4 (April 1974)
      24-33.

      The author believes that the notion of "public trust"
      still has meaning and deserves to be emphasized in educating
      public servants indeed, the absurdity of public
      administration procedures (caused by limited and fragmented
      authority as well as secrecy) requires concentrated
      "thought, skill and effort."

122. Chandler, Ralph Clark. "The Problem of Moral Reasoning in
      American Public Administration: The Case for a Code of
      Ethics." Public Administration Review 43, 1
      (January-February 1983) 32-39.

      The arguments for and against a code of ethics among
      public administrators (represented here by the American
      Society for Public Administration) are summarized,
      categorized, and analyzed. There are three negative: 1)
      practicality; 2) procedure; and 3) administrative theory
      (the value neutral administrator has no discretion and hence
      no moral responsibility); and three positive: 1)
      objectivism (transcendent values exist; actions are the
      predicates of being); 2) community (the community is the
      arbiter of ethics and ethical relativism represents both a
      loss of paradigm and a loss of community in public
      administration); and 3) courage (the language of moral
      choice enables that which in any case is necessary).

123. Chandler, Ralph Clark. "The Problem of Moral Illiteracy in
      Professional Discourse: The Case of the Statement of
      Principles of the American Society for Public
      Administration." American Review of Public
      Administration 16, 4 (Winter 1982) 369-386.

      In 1981, the American Society for Public Administration
      rejected a proposed code of ethics. The historical reasons
      behind this are seen as an outgrowth of the American values
      of liberty and prosperity free of moral coercion. The text
      of the code is presented, as is the text of a statement of
      principles which was adopted later. While the code spoke of
      transcendent values, the principles dealt with relative
      ethics, eschewing moral language and symbols, a sense of

community, or courage and beauty. The Weberian morally neutral administrator is no longer a valid model since the Nuremberg trials. Therefore, the Society must recognize this reality and adopt an enforceable ethical code.

124. Clarke, James Patrick. Codes of Ethics and Public Service. Ph.D. Dissertation, New York University (1965).

In view of continuing ethics problems in government and the ineffectiveness of law as a control over abuse of public office, this dissertation discusses the governmental code of ethics as an administrative solution to these problems. The public officer, as a professional and by law, has a fiduciary responsibility to place the public interest above his own interests. Yet conflict of interest is a fact of life in the United States, affecting both government and business, and is a proper concern of public administration.

The dissertation concludes that government in the United States should consider development of codes of ethics as an administrative solution to ethical problems inherent in government, rather than relying on traditional, severe and consequently little-used conflict of interest statutes present in most governmental jurisdictions in the United States. The study also contains conclusions about the content and administration of a governmental code of ethics, the applicability of a code of ethics to all branches of government and its relationship to law and the profession of public administration. The dissertation further states that public administration must assert its interest in and its capacity to contribute to the development and administration of codes of ethics potentially applicable to the 9,000,000 civilian employees of government in the United States, if the code of ethics is to be a viable instrument.

125. Danielson, James L., and Russ Smith. "The Application of Regression Analysis to Equality and Merit in Personnel Decisions." Public Personnel Management 10, 1 (1981).

A political culture defines the boundaries of public notice. The development of the democratic tradition in America, although placing great importance on the value of equality is marked by varying interpretations of the concept. Since the mid-1960's, Congress has enacted several laws to end discrimination in hiring, compensation, and other aspects of employment. Despite these actions, women, racial minorities, handicapped workers, and other protected groups have not always reaped the benefits of equal employment opportunity. This may not lie entirely in the hands of employers who act unlawfully. Unfortunately, personnel officers are expected to apply the principle of equality in a political culture that sends "mixed signals." Implementation of the goal of equality has been hindered by the twin problems of precisely defining "equal treatment" and assessing the magnitude of "disparate treatment." A brief examination of the principles of equality and merit helps us understand the context within which these problems arise.

Equality is an abstract, though broadly agreed-upon value in our culture. The more specific application of that value often takes the form of such concepts as equal opportunity, equal treatment and equal pay for equal work. The personnel officer is faced with the task of applying the equality principle to concrete situations involving promotion and compensation in a system designed to operate according to the merit principle.

The statistical technique of stepwise regression analysis can be used to describe a situation within an organization and then identify individuals for whom the principle of equal pay for equal work is violated. Also, appropriate remedial action is suggested by the technique, enabling the personnel officer to make an ethical decision consistent with both the broad values of equality and merit. The technique, then, can aid administrators in acting as ethical agents within the broad guidelines provided by the American political culture and the general language of legislation.

126. Denhardt, Kathryn. "Toward a More Ethical Public Administration," Ph.D. Dissertation, University of Kansas (1984).

The development of an ethical framework for the field of public administration ethics has seemingly lacked a coherent conceptualization of what it means to be an ethical administrator. By examining the approaches of various writers during the past half century as well as philosophical literature on ethics, a conceptualization is developed which incorporates those approaches and which attempts to be both practicable and philosophically sound.

The conceptualization is analyzed through an examination of the social and historical context of public administration (including the moral construct of the society) as well as the organizational context within which

public administrators function. This study draws upon
literature in philosophy, applied ethics, and organization
theory (among others) and helps to illuminate the ways in
which the social and organizational contexts provide
supports for, or constraints on, ethical administration.
Then, possibilities for enhancing ethics within individuals
and within organizations are discussed.

The analysis and concluding case study lead to the
recommendation that aspects of the education and
socialization of public administrators, as well as factors
associated with organizations need to be reformed in order
to enhance ethical deliberation among public administrators.

127. Dennis, Jr., Harry C. "Standards for PA Education."
     Bureaucrat 13, 1 (Spring 1984) 29-36.

     A critique of the education offered prospective public
     administrators is presented. A quantitative and qualitative
     survey is reviewed, the qualitative survey considering such
     benefits as analytical skills, management skills,
     communication skills, knowledge of the environments,
     knowledge of organizations, and budgeting and public
     finance, and such shortcomings and proposed changes as a
     dearth of quantitative skills, and lack of federal emphasis,
     future orientation, and a teaching of values and ethics.

128. Douglas, Paul H. Ethics in Government. Cambridge, Mass.:
     Harvard University Press (1951).

     Summarizes Douglas' thoughts on ethical problems and
     solutions based on his experiences "as alderman...on the
     Chicago City Council and then as a United States Senator."
     The examples in "Ethical Problems of Administrators"
     (Chapter 2, pp. 27-63) are historically dated but the
     substance of the remarks is timely.

129. Dwivedi, O. P., and Ernest A. Engelbert. "Education and
     Training for Values and Ethics in the Public Service: An
     International Perspective." Public Personnel Management
     10, 1 (1981) 140-145.

     During the last five years the International Association
     of Schools and Institutes of Administration (IASIA) has
     devoted a considerable portion of its activities to an
     examination of values and ethics in education and training
     programs for public administration/public management
     (PA/PM). Two of the five working groups of the Association

have been involved with this subject. International
investigations of the content of ethics programs in schools
and institutes have been conducted, reports prepared, and
curriculum guidelines and standards for education and
training programs have been adopted.

Inasmuch as representatives of greatly contrasting
political and cultural systems participated in the
deliberations, opinions were highly diverse and fraught with
controversy. However, from the commencement of the
Association's discussions, the view prevailed among the
working groups that this subject could not be ignored in
education and training programs for those nations concerned
with quality of the public service.

This paper briefly reviews the experience of IASIA in
undertaking the complex and thorny task of incorporating
values and ethics into education and training programs for
PA/PM. The first section highlights some of the overriding
conceptual issues which cut across the Association's
deliberations. The next section presents some of the
findings of an international survey concerning the
availability of education and government service training
programs in public responsibility. The content of
curriculum guidelines and standards adopted by IASIA are
detailed in the third part. The concluding section denotes
some of the elements for achieving an effective education
and training program for values and ethics in public
administration/public management.

130. Embry, Charles R. "Ethics and Public Administration." News
      for Teachers of Political Science 42 (Summer 1984).

This is an excellent article which develops an ethics
course for Public Administration built around the role of
the humanities. His objective is to develop a course which
would involve philosophical questioning and thinking in
general, and moral thinking in particular. He prepares a
course which makes the students aware of the ethical
dimension of decision-making. He provides a reading list
and course outline for the students.

131. Evans, James W. "A New Administrative Ethic?: Attitudes of
      Public Managers and Students." Public Personnel
      Management 10, 1 (1981) 132-139.

In the United States, ethical questions are typically
addressed on two levels. One level is personal ethics, also

known as internal ethics. This involves the rightness and
wrongness of individual behavior in interaction with other
people. The focus is on organizational members: How is a
person to be treated? How is a person to treat others? The
second level concerns the actions of institutions and
organizations in society and is known as social, or external
ethics. The concern is with the organization's clients:
How are they to be treated? What is fair? Ethics, then, is
concerned primarily with the impact of decisions on people
within and without organizations, individually and
collectively. Any action which has a present or potential
impact on human beings involves ethics. Human well-being
and personal dignity are fundamental ethical concepts. Also
fundamental is the responsibility a person has for the human
outcomes of any conscious, freely willed act. In sum,
ethics is conduct that is fair, just, and right.

To assure ethical behavior, standards and codes of proper
conduct are erected at various times by institutions and
organizations. Though these codes may be amended as social
mores change, their main thrust remains compatible with
Judeo-Christian ethics as presented in teleological and
de-ontological ethical theories. What the written standards
imply is that no person is to seek private gain at another's
expense (i.e., misrepresentation, bribes, kickbacks, payoffs,
opportune investments, and so on). Exploitation of others
is also judged as unethical.

With respect to governmental affairs, ethical behavior is
traditionally defined as behavior which is honest,
efficient, in the public interest, and consistent with
utilitarian precepts of doing the greatest good for the
greatest number. Thus, ethical individuals, or
organizations, would never engage in fraudulent, wasteful,
or abusive behavior. Abusive behavior is behavior in which
an official position is used to seek personal advantage at
the expense of another person, or the public at large.

This research elucidated fundamental differences in
ethical and ideological beliefs that may explain some of the
difficulty public organizations have in establishing
consistent ethical behavior among their employees.

132. Fleishman, Joel L. and others, ed. Public Duties: The
Moral Obligations of Government Officials. Cambridge,
Mass: Harvard University Press (1981).

Based on seminars conducted by the Faculty Study Group on

the Moral Obligations of Public Officials, under the
auspices of the Institute of Politics, John F. Kennedy
School of Government, Harvard University.

133. Fox, Charles J. "Civil Service Reform and Ethical
Accountability." Public Personnel Management 10, 1
(1981) 98-102.

One important issue which emerges from the current wave
of civil service reform has to do with the locus of ethical
agency--the authority to interpret the public interest and
act upon it. In a democracy, ethical public service, if it
means anything at all, means behavior consistent with the
public interest. But what is the public interest?
Actually, it is the modern secular equivalent of what
political philosophers once took to be natural law or higher
law. In one sense "the public interest" is rather like an
improbable but nonetheless indispensable legal fiction. In
another sense the public interest is an important background
norm which shapes the discretionary decisions of public
servants. The question raised by civil service reform is
what mediates between the norm and the activity? How are
acts made accountable to norms? What is the appropriate
source of the power and responsibility to interpret the
ethical manifestations of "the public interest?" Two polar
positions may be identified on this issue which can be
termed unilateralism and multilaterism. Should ethical
agencies reside at the apex of institutional command
(unilateralism) or should it be diffused to line
functionaries (multilateralism)? The author analyzes these
two points of view.

134. Frankel, Mark S. "Ethics and Responsibility in Political
Science Research." International Social Science Journal
30, 1 (1978) 173-180.

The requirements of access and disclosure, as they relate
to studies of the behavior and institutions of government,
have generated controversy over research ethics and
responsibility wherever social science research is
conducted. The controversy is complicated by the highly
sensitive subject matter which is frequently the focus of
investigation in political science. The issues in dispute
include: (1) the public's right to know, (2) citizen
demands for efficient and responsive public institutions,
(3) the government's responsibility to protect the national
interest, (4) the need to assure citizens' rights to
privacy, and (5) the scholar's responsibility to seek

knowledge and improve understanding without compromising the
methods of science. The issues are discussed in the context
of two different models of the researcher-subject
relationship. The "easy-access model," which is borrowed
from medical research, is of limited relevance for it
presumes that the investigator possesses power and knowledge
that can intimidate his subjects. But in studies of
political power, vested interests and institutional
pathology, the political scientist is often in a position of
social subordination and political dependency vis-a-vis his
subjects. The "reciprocity model," however, recognizes the
importance of a partnership between scholars and government
in political science research and provides a more useful
framework for analyzing and assessing the trade-offs
involved in balancing value conflicts and serving the public
interest. In assessing the ethics dilemmas which surface
during the investigation of government institutions and
public policies, a 1975 survey of 36 national political
science associations found that only 3 had initiated action
to develop principles of conduct for researchers. Proposals
for standards and revisions of research policies are
presented.

135. Gilbert, Charles S. "The Framework of Administrative
      Responsibility." Journal of Politics 21, 3 (August 1959)
      373-407.

      After identifying and analyzing varying uses of the term
"administrative responsibility" in the literature, Gilbert
uses the "internal-external" and "formal-informal"
dichotomies both to classify institutional patterns
suggested by others as means of controlling responsibility
and to raise a number of questions for further
investigation.

136. Graceffa, John P. "Ethical Considerations of the Federal
      Lawyer Upon Entering Private Practice." Western New
      England Law Review 4 (Fall 1981) 199-222.

      In recent years, government employment has provided the
law school graduate with a legal apprenticeship more common
to an earlier era. Although such practical experience is
advantageous, there are some unseen aspects of government
employment that should be considered by the neophyte lawyer.
The lawyer entering government service should look not only
to the present but also to the future when he will be
entering or reentering private practice. The purpose of
this article is to explore the ethical considerations facing

the government lawyer about to enter private practice. Similar considerations apply to the new lawyer presently contemplating government service. Particular attention will be given to the conflicting public policies that arise whenever courts consider the ethical problems encountered by a government lawyer entering private practice. The article then will examine the approaches frequently employed to maintain a balance between these conflicting policies.

It also is important to remember that ethical rules are largely a function of historical developments and changing social mores. Thus, ethical standards should not be etched in stone. Rather, ethical standards should remain flexible so that they can conform to prevailing societal values.

137. Graham, George A. "Ethical Guidelines for Public Administrators: Observation on Rules of the Game." Public Administration Review 34 (January-February 1974) 90-92.

Recognizing that the public administrator is most seriously tried by "conflicting obligations and loyalties" Graham organizes his guidelines under what he considers to be the most difficult issues for the administrator: his "input to decisions," "the limits of compromise," and the actual implementation of decisions.

An experienced administrator learns in time that the most serious and difficult ethical problems arise out of conflicts of loyalty and conflicts of involvements, activities, and commitments outside of his job which would bias his judgment on the job or reduce his motivation to do a good job in the public interest.

Conflicts of loyalty tend to be more difficult to contain. They result from the growing size and complexity of governmental organizations, the wide range and interaction of governmental functions, and the necessary practice of vesting discretion in officials at various points and many levels of the governmental organization. This delegation of discretion is authorized by law on the assumption that it will be exercised wisely and in good faith, and it is done because it is necessary in order to secure high performance. The administrative system that has evolved thus rests equally on a foundation of professional competence and personal integrity.

Where there is discretion, there is uncertainty, and

there may be conflicting obligations and loyalties. In dealing with this situation, the administrator is subject to a double hierarchy of authority, one impersonal and one personal, which defines his obligations. The hierarchy of law (constitutional, statutory, administrative) is impersonal. The chain of direction or command, into which he fits somewhere, is quite personal. The law in its various forms frequently is stated in general terms, which must be interpreted, and administered.

This article prescribes the administrator's role in a democratic society to insure ethical behavior.

138. Gross, John H. "Ethics In Government Act - Major Provisions 'Unfair.'" New York Law Journal 87 (June 29, 1982) 2.

The author argues that the Post Watergate reform legislation has been a double edged sword. Whatever else can be said of this legislation, it had the desired effect of restricting the scope of executive action. In fact, in many important areas, such as law enforcement, the Executive Branch found itself impeded in effectively pursuing wholly legitimate ends. He cited the example of the tax reform act of 1976 which put controls on the I.R.S. to share information in its files with other parts of government for any purpose.

This essay will focus on the unique position of the congressional staff attorney as an unelected representative of the legislative branch. In order to address the ethical issues and problems faced by congressional staff attorneys, this essay examines ethical questions associated with accountability, guidelines and standards, and the political process. Specifically, four basic questions will be addressed:

1. To whom is the congressional staff attorney accountable, and what impact does this question and political partisanship have on ethical decision making?
2. What legal and ethical codes currently guide the congressional staff attorney, and how effective are they?
3. How does the congressional environment affect ethical decision making and are the pressures faced in Congress unique from those facing legal practitioners outside of Capitol Hill?
4. What can be done to improve or clarify the appropriate ethical standards for congressional staff

attorneys?

139. Hill, James P. "Ethics for the Unelected." American Bar
     Association Journal 68 (August 1982) 950-954.

     This article is directed toward an attorney who chose
     Capitol Hill for a career. The author suggests that the
     most serious challenge they will face deals with the
     question of accountability, not legal competence. Hill
     raises four basic questions: (1) To whom is the
     congressional staff attorney accountable? (2) What legal
     and ethical codes currently guide the congressional staff?
     (3) How does the congressional environment affect ethical
     decisions? and (4) What can be done to improve ethical
     standards?

140. Howe, Elizabeth, and Jerome Kaufman. "Ethics and
     Professional Practice in Planning and Related Policy
     Professions." Policy Studies Journal 9, 4 (1980-1981)
     585-595.

     Ethical principles in professions can be related either
     to ends or to means. Here, attitudes about the ethics of
     means among urban planners are explored. A variety of means
     are classified into a hierarchy, from the most to the least
     ethical, and differences in responses to the hierarchy
     explored. Implications for other public policy fields are
     also discussed.

141. Jonsen, Albert R., and Lewis H. Butler. "Public Ethics and
     Policy Making." The Hasting Center Report 5 (August
     1975) 19-31.

     The authors believe that "public ethics" can be most
     useful to policy makers, not by supplying the relationships
     among a "vague affinity of concept, but by centering ethical
     arguments on the specific policy debate and clarifying the
     moral principles and tradeoffs involved in the
     decision-making process.

142. Kefauver, Estes. "Past and Present Standards of Public
     Ethics in America: Are We Improving?" Annals of the
     American Academy of Political and Social Science 280
     (March 1952) 1-8.

     This historical piece places responsibility for
     encouraging and maintaining high standards of conduct within
     the public service squarely on the shoulders of the

citizenry.

143. Kernaghan, Kenneth. "Codes of Ethics and Administrative
      Responsibility." Canadian Public Administration 17
      (Winter 1974) 527-541.

      Advocating the use of a code of ethics as an effective
      way to "promote" administrative responsibility, Kernaghan
      explores the advantages and disadvantages (pros and cons) of
      codes—particularly the problems of content and enforcement.
      He concludes that the ideal would be a "self-enforcing"
      code, one which is internalized by employees and manifested
      through personal example and influence.

144. Kernaghan, Kenneth. "Codes of Ethics and Public
      Administration: Progress, Problems and Prospects."
      Public Administration 59 (Summer 1980) 207-223.

      This article examines regulations governing the ethical
      conduct of public employees in Canada and discusses the
      administration of them.

      This paper focuses on the conduct of appointed officials.
      Attention is centered on Canadian governments but references
      are made to developments elsewhere and most of my
      observations are directly applicable to ethical issues in
      other countries. Also, emphasis is placed primarily, but
      not exclusively, on those ethical problem areas most
      troublesome in Canada, the United States, Britain and
      Australia—namely conflicts of interest, confidentiality,
      political partisanship and public comment.

145. Kintner, Earl W. "Legal Limitations and Possibilities for
      Self-Enforcement of Codes of Ethics." The Ethical Basis
      on Economic Freedom Ivan Hill (ed.) Chapel Hill, N.C.:
      American Viewpoint (1976) 387-402.

      Although Kintner agrees with others that internalizing
      codes of ethics is the best way to insure ethical behavior
      by all, he gives an overview of some of the drawbacks as
      well as advantages in establishing specific codes.

146. Kneier, Andrew. "Ethics in Government Service." The
      Ethical Basis of Economic Freedom Ivan Hill (ed.) Chapel
      Hill, N.C.: American Viewpoint (1976) 215-232.

      Kneier discusses the public vs. private interest
      tradeoffs which have always been problems for government

workers and concludes that tough conflict of interest laws are needed.

147. Kreutzer, S. Stanley. "Protecting the Public Service: A National Ethics Commission." National Civic Review 64 (July 1975) 339-342.

An address to the National Municipal League's annual meeting in November, 1974, in which the author calls for a national commission on ethics to provide guidelines and advisors' opinions and to initiate proceedings. At the same time, he stresses the importance of personal integrity and the counter-productive impact of requiring full financial disclosure by all individuals seeking public office.

148. Lawry, Robert P. "Confidences and the Government Lawyer." North Carolina Law Review 57 (May 1979) 625-646.

The author addresses the issue of whether the Cannon of Ethics as a moral code should govern the activities of all lawyers and all lawyering jobs. He suggests that considerable differences exist among the kinds of ethical problems encountered by lawyers doing probate work, or criminal work, or contract negotiating or litigation.

The question raised is whether there ought to be different ethical rules and standards governing the behavior of lawyers, depending on the nature of the lawyer's practice. The author suggests changes to address an immediate problem in one of the Cannons. He calls for debate and discussion which would lead to other proposed changes.

149. Levitan, David M. "The Responsibility of Administrative Officials in a Democratic Society." Political Science Quarterly 61, 4 (December 1946) 562-598.

Assuming the continuance of existing external controls, Levitan argues for such internal improvements as better recruitment and education of public servants.

This article examines the question of the responsibility of the Civil Service under a democratic system of government. The author attempts to analyze the position of the administrative official under our constitutional system. He concludes that our success in the quest for a responsible democracy will depend upon our ability to foster respect and devotion to representative institutions.

150. Leys, Wayne A.R. "Ethics and Administrative Discretion."
     Public Administration Review 3, 1 (Winter 1943) 10-23.

     Concerned with administrative choices which establish
     standards for the public, Leys believes that by
     distinguishing legislative grants of discretionary power
     into three categories (such as prescribing a rule, social
     planning, and political mediation), the philosophical
     dialogue on ethics can be more meaningful than that of the
     legal perspective.

151. Longmire, Dennis R. "Ethical Dilemmas in the Research
     Setting: A Survey of Experiences and Responses in the
     Criminological Community." Criminology 21, 3 (August
     1983) 333-348.

     The frequency with which criminological researchers are
     confronted with various ethical dilemmas is ascertained
     through a questionnaire survey of 191 members of the
     American Society of Criminology. The results reveal that
     approximately 63% of those criminologists who have been
     active in research since 1975 have experienced one or more
     of eight types of ethical dilemmas. Further analysis
     demonstrates that criminologists favor developing a
     professional code of conduct as well as some legal
     guidelines in this area. The majority of those surveyed do
     not believe governmental regulations or a general sense of
     morality among the researchers are effective mechanisms in
     preventing ethical dilemmas.

152. Mance, Barbara G. "Toward A New Ethical Standard Regulating
     the Private Practice of Former Government Lawyers."
     Golden Gate University Law Review 13 (Spring 1983)
     433-460.

     This article addresses the 1978 legislation dealing with
     former government lawyers in the Ethics in Government Act.
     This article advocates the elimination of the appearance of
     impropriety as a legal and ethical standard governing the
     disqualification of former government lawyers and urges the
     ABA to adopt Rule 1.11 which would provide a comprehensible,
     precise ethical rule regulating the post-government
     practices of lawyers in conformity with federal statute and
     regulation.

153. Morstein Marx, Fritz. "Administrative Ethics and the Rule
     of Law." American Political Science Review 43 (December

1949) 119-1144.

Marx believes that "the core of all administrative ethics lies in the ideas that nourish the political system" and that, by examining such basic premises as "a government of laws, not men" and our belief in the "common good," public administration should be able to derive some general norms of conduct which, when interfaced with "rules of law," will provide ethical guidelines.

154. Maskell, Jack. "Ethics Manual for Members and Employees of the U.S. House of Representatives." United States House Committee on Standards of Official Conduct. Washington, DC: 96th Congress, 1st session (1979).

155. Monypenny, Phillip. "A Code of Ethics as a Means of Controlling Administrative Conduct." Public Administration Review 13, 3 (Summer 1953) 184-187.

One of the first articles in Public Administration Review to suggest the need for a Code of Ethics. The article reviews the developments surrounding the Ethics Standards in Government Report of the 82nd Congress. Furthermore, the paper suggests a code of ethics for public employees as a means of controlling administrative behavior. He suggests that an ethical code would be an important device for administrative control useful in reducing systematic statements to the highest standards of behavior.

156. Murphy, William L. "Vicarious Disqualification of Government Lawyers." American Bar Association Journal 69 (March 1983) 299-303.

The author addresses when the American Bar Association's Code of Ethics requires lawyers to withdraw for a case. Designed to protect the clients and the lawyers, the ABA code generally prevents a breach of trust or wrongful disclosure by preventing the situation where it may occur. The article suggests that lawyers in public service are subject to the same rules as all other lawyers. The article focuses on the proposed model of Professional Conduct. He is somewhat critical of the new proposal because a lawyer could be chosen to head a government legal office not because of skill or knowledge, but because of lack of experience.

157. O'Keefe, Constance, and Peter Safirstein. "Fallen Angels, Separation of Powers, and the Saturday Night Massacre:

An Examination of the Practical, Constitutional, and
Political Tensions in the Special Prosecutor Provisions
of the Ethics in Government Act." Brooklyn Law Review 49
(Fall 1982) 113-147.

The Ethics in Government Act of 1978 (the Act or the
Ethics Act) was enacted by Congress "to preserve and promote
the accountability and integrity of public officials and of
the institutions of the Federal Government." By providing
for the appointment of temporary prosecutors who act
virtually free of control by the executive branch, the
Special Prosecutor provisions of the Act were designed to
insure thorough, unbiased investigations of alleged
violations of federal law by high-level government
officials. These provisions of the Act are subject to a
sunset provision and will expire on October 26, 1983. On
August 12, 1982, the Senate passed a bill introduced by
Senator William S. Cohen of Maine to amend and extend the
Special Prosecutor provisions; the House subcommittee to
which the bill was then referred held hearings but took no
action on it before Congress adjourned on October 2, 1982.
Thus, as of the date of this writing, the future of the
Special Prosecutor legislation is uncertain.

Since their enactment, the Special Prosecutor provisions
have been criticized both on constitutional and policy
grounds. This article assesses the validity of that
criticism and the wisdom of the proposed amendments, and
will conclude with the authors' own suggestions as to the
form in which the Special Prosecutor legislation should be
re-enacted.

158. Parsons, Anne. "Professional and Individual Ethics With
     Respect to Policy Research: A Comment on 'The Growing
     Demand for Behavioral Science in Government' and
     Rejoinder." New Haven, CT Human Organization 23, 2
     (Summer 1964) 93-95, 97-98.

In this short research note the author responds to an
article concerning Professional Ethics in the field of
Applied Anthropology. The author has three main ethical
concerns about the discipline; to focus on (1) formulating
general theories or explanations; (2) formulating specific
questions; (3) gathering information in the field. The
author suggests that there are times when the makers of
policy have motives that are not consistent with the trust
placed in them.

159. Rainey, Hal G. "Reward Preferences Among Public and Private
     Managers: In Search of the Service Ethic." American
     Review of Public Administration 16, 4 (Winter 1982)
     288-302.

     The work-related values and reward preferences of public
     and private middle managers were investigated. Previous
     studies on this subject are reviewed, as are the sampling
     and analytical procedures. Public service was the main
     difference between the value systems of the two groups,
     found largely among public agency employees. There was
     considerable overlap on such questions as pay, status, and
     prestige. The study shows that, although money is important
     to public sector employees, another important incentive for
     them is a sense of social service. These motives, however,
     are often vague. To clarify this topic, further work on
     professionalism, public administration ethics,
     organizational commitment and altruism is recommended.

160. Riggs, R. Richard. "The Professionalization of the Public
     Service: A Roadmap for the 1980s and Beyond." American
     Review of Public Administration 16, 4 (Winter 1982)
     349-369.

     The components of professionalism are defined and
     explained: 1) a body of knowledge; 2) primary community
     orientation; 3) a professional organization; 4)
     licensure and a code of ethics; 5) a monopoly on practice;
     6) community sanction; and 7) autonomy. Public
     administration has a body of expertise and several nascent
     organizations, but still lacks a licensing procedure, a
     binding ethical code, or a community orientation.

     To fully professionalize, public administrators must
     consolidate, bargain for monopoly and autonomy, and obtain
     community sanction. The specific steps in each process are
     outlined.

161. Rohr, John A. "The Problem of Professional Ethics."
     Bureaucrat 11, 2 (Summer 1982) 47-50.

     While codes of professional ethics are expressed in
     universal principles, professional life involves specific
     cases which may require deviation from commonly accepted
     moral standards in the interest of a higher good. The
     political manipulation of the career civil service is a
     violation of the professionalism of government employees.
     It is argued that the resistance of improper political

influence means the establishment of professional autonomy and that this is for the public welfare. The grounds for such autonomy for public administrators, however, are less clear than for other elite professions such as medicine and the law.

162. Rohr, John A. "Ethics for Bureaucrats." America 128, 26 (May 1973) 488-491.

Rohr blames the "science-politics" dichotomy in public administration (in part) for the failure of bureaucrats to accept themselves as policy makers who need to "reflect on the moral dimension of their activity." He sees educational institutions, including churches, as part of the remedy.

163. Rohr, John A. Ethics for Bureaucrats: An Essay on Law and Values. New York: Marcel Dekker (1978).

Focusing on the problem of "how to integrate the study of ethics in the curricula of schools of public administration and centers for public management training," Rohr provides an overview of the dilemmas facing bureaucrats, the perspective of philosophers and scholars in the past and a suggestion for preparing bureaucrats for the present and future. His own bias toward law is evident in his conclusion that "the method of regime values proposed the Constitution of the U.S. as the most appropriate focal point for normative reflection by American bureaucrats."

164. Rohr, John A. "The Study of Ethics in the PA Curriculum." Public Administration Review 36, 4 (July-August 1976) 398-406.

This article offers a preliminary and more succinct statement of his "regime values" approach to ethics described in his book Ethics for Bureaucrats. He also outlines his argument against including traditional study of ethics in the curriculum or using the "new PA" concept of "social equity" as the foundation for bureaucratic ethics.

The author outlines a method for integrating the study of ethics into public administration curriculum. The article begins by examining the normative implication that arises from administrative discretion and the relationship between such discretion and the political role of the bureaucrat. There follows a criticism of the tendency of "new" public administration literature to rely upon political philosophy and humanistic psychology as the foundations for ethical reflections. The author argues against political philosophy because it is too demanding to be included as part of a course in ethics, and he argues against humanistic psychology because it necessarily focuses upon the individual as a person rather than upon his chosen career. As an alternative to these two, it is suggested that, since students of public administration aspire to positions of leadership within the bureaucracy of a particular regime, the values of that regime are the most suitable starting point for their ethical reflections. The argument for this method is rooted in the obligation of bureaucrats in a democratic polity to use their discretionary power in a manner that is consistent with the values of the people in whose name they govern. The author goes on to explain how American students of public administration might best go about systematically reflecting on the values of the present republic. Two tasks are described: 1) Identify American values; 2) Look for meaningful statements about them.

165. Rohr, John A. "Ethics For the Senior Executive Service: Suggestions for Management Training." Administration and Society 12, 2 (August- 1980) 203-216.

Considered as a showcase of the 1978 Civil Service Reform Act, the Senior Executive Service (SES) has come under fire on the grounds that its establishment may politicize the higher levels of the U.S. civil service. This article examines the issue, and recognizes the potential for improper political influence in institutions such as the SES. As one remedy, the author proposes the development of an ethics-in-management training program for higher level civil servants based on the following training devices: 1) the oath of office; 2) institutional literacy; and 3) Presidential politics. This type of training program is seen as promoting political neutrality, loyalty to the United States Constitution and the rule of law, and professionalism in the bureaucracy.

166. Rosenbloom, David H. "Public Administrative Professionalism and Public Service Law." State and Local Government Review 16, 2 (Spring 1984) 52-57.

The growth of government at all levels has focused attention upon the behavior of public service personnel and the potential for abuse of the public interest. The role of professionalism has been debated, stressing internal or external means of control. Bureaucratic values of efficiency and economy have often clashed with the democratic constitutional values of individuality, equity, and procedural fairness. Professional education is a major vehicle for the development of professionalism compatible with democratic constitutionalism. Three particularly salient areas are: 1) public employees' liability for unconstitutional activities; 2) the right to disobey an unethical order; and 3) whistleblowing.

167. Sayre, Wallace S. "Trends of a Decade in Administrative Values." Public Administration Review 11, 1 (Winter 1951) 1-9.

Sayre reviews some of the important publications and reports of the decade and concludes that "the sense of the importance of values in public administration has increased significantly during the decade.... The continuing debate on this score is about the relative importance of 'facts' and 'values' and about the usefulness of this distinction in the study and practice of administration."

168. Scheiber, Walter A. "The ICMA Code of Ethics." Public Management 57, 6 (June 1975) 15-16.

This article is an examination of the ICMA Code of Ethics. The author provides an excellent history and description of the ICMA Committee on Professional Conduct. The article provides insight into the composition, methods of operation, and procedural issues of the committee.

One difficult issue is the question of how to deal with allegations of ethical wrongdoing on the part of non-members.

169. Sherwood, Frank P. "Professional Ethics." Public Management 57 (June 1975) 13-14.

A brief analysis of the limited usefulness of codes of ethics, stressing instead the importance of social and organizational processes which provide opportunities for considering the "value dimension."

170. Sikula, Andrew. "The Values and Value Systems of Government Executives." Public Personnel Management 2 (January-February 1973) 16-22.

Based on a subsample of government executives working for HEW in the Midwest region, Sikula found support in survey responses for his theory that "personalities within certain

occupations and careers have unique values and value system
characteristics" which could have implications for job
placement, training programs, etc. His respondents were
exclusively males with two or more years of experience and
ranked at GS 14 or above. They rated most highly as
terminal goals, family security, self-respect,
accountability, freedom, and equality. The instrumental
characteristics most highly valued were honesty,
responsibility, capability, helpfulness, and self-control.

171. Sommers, Christina Hoff. "Ethics Without Virtue: Moral
     Education in America." The American Scholar 53, 3
     (Summer 1984) 381-389.

Examining recent trends in United States moral education,
education movements such as Sidney Simon's values
clarification and Lawrence Kohlberg's cognitive moral
development, as well as the new "applied ethics" movement in
colleges, are discussed and criticized for lacking moral
substance. Large numbers of United States students in
elementary and secondary schools are not becoming acquainted
with the Western moral tradition; serious study of the moral
classics has been replaced by gimmicky and empirically
dubious classroom "dialogues" and "strategies" that tend to
encourage narcissism and ethical relativism. The applied
ethics trend in the colleges is an important and welcome
development, but its emphasis is primarily on the
responsibilities of corporations, hospitals, schools, and
governments; discussion of the moral responsibilities of the
student is avoided out of fear of indoctrination, and the
moral value of wisdom, courage, honesty, and compassion is
all but ignored. These general developments in United
States education that ignore traditional morality and
deemphasize personal integrity are termed "ethics without
virtue."

172. Stahl, Glenn O. "Democracy and Public Employee Morality."
     Annals of the American Academy of Political and Social
     Science 297 (January 1955) 90-97.

Emphasizing the unique obligation of civil servants
always to be aware of "the public interest," Stahl
recommends that the "moral base of public administration" be
strengthened through upgrading the educational focus on
ethics, standard-setting by government leaders, increased
agency communication with the public, and more recognition
and reward by the public when distinguished service is
rendered by a public employee.

173. Stahl, Glenn O. "Public Service Ethics in a Democracy."
      Public Personnel Administration, 7th edition. New York:
      Harper and Row (1976).

      A cursory review of some of the important issues such as
      conflict of interest, expertise and legal codes versus
      individual integrity. Stahl comes down firmly on the side
      of developing and rewarding pride in public service rather
      than relying on legalistic restrictions.

174. Thayer, Fred C. "Civil Service Reform and Performance
      Appraisal: A Policy Disaster." Public Personnel
      Management 10, 1 (1981) 20-28.

      The recent civil service reform, introduced by Jimmy
      Carter as both "the most sweeping reform of the Civil
      Service System since it was created nearly 100 years ago,"
      and "the centerpiece of government reorganization during my
      term in office," swept through Congress with overwhelming
      support from both political parties and the general public.
      Since more than 1500 individuals and groups inside and
      outside government were involved in drawing up the reform,
      it is clear that the most "enlightened" students of
      administration were just as enthusiastic. There is no
      indication that this general support has lessened since
      passage of the reform, but scattered problems and questions
      are emerging and, as I see it, these can only increase. To
      put it briefly, the reform's viability is almost wholly
      dependent upon periodic performance appraisals of career
      administrators, based solely upon "merit" and "competence,"
      never upon "subjective," "personal," or "political"
      considerations. No matter how laudable this purpose may be,
      and no matter how much effort may be expended by
      conscientious supervisors and personnel managers, the
      purpose cannot be achieved.

      The purpose here is to outline why performance appraisal
      systems do not and cannot work.

175. Wakefield, Susan. "Ethics and Public Service: A Case for
      Individual Responsibility." Public Administration Review
      36, 6 (November-December, 1976) 661-666.

      Awarded the ASPA Grant Garvey Student Manuscript Award in
      1975, this essay stresses the need for development of
      "internal commitment to moral government" through education
      of current and future public servants.

176. Wise, Daniel. "Federal Judge Stresses Ethics of Lawyers for Governments." (New York) New York Law Review 92 (November 21, 1984) 3.

   In a short note, the author states that Government attorneys, like CPA's are public lawyers and have an ethical obligation to be among the "chief whistle-blowers" of the Government. He states that there are circumstances where the government attorney "must stand up to his client in the interests of a larger client--what the attorney conceives to be the proper service of the law, of the public interest, or of morality."

   Reviewing the applicable provisions of the Code of Professional Responsibility, the Rules of Civil Procedure and fee-award statutes, Judge Weinstein concluded government attorneys have an ethical responsibility to exercise "independent judgment." To do otherwise, he suggested, and "postulate a public lawyer slavishly obedient to the government's or an agency's policies" would "create a sense of grave discomfort."

177. Worthley, John A., and Barbara R. Grumet. "Ethics and Public Administration: Teaching What 'Can't Be Taught.'" American Review of Public Administration 17, 1 (Spring 1983) 54-67.

   The difficulty of teaching ethics in public administration is assessed, and an alternative approach, used successfully at several university test sites, is described and discussed. Existing approaches to the subject are reviewed first, and can be summarized as four: 1) analysis of "horror" stories such as Watergate, with a fairly clear right-wrong element; 2) study of codes of conduct; 3) emphasis on law: ethics is avoiding the illegal, or that which gets you sued, or fired; and 4) study of the great philosophers. The authors propose a phenomenological approach to teaching the subject, discuss its format and objectives, and present its outline, a case illustration, and include an appendix with a selected bibliography of relevant teaching materials. These are the stated objectives of the course: 1) to develop and broaden awareness and appreciation of the power of the public servant, the values of the public service system, and the ethical dimensions of public service; 2) to provide understanding of the mechanisms of accountability and controls in public service; and 3) to assist public service professionals in developing operational guidelines for ethical behavior.

178. Worthley, John A. "Ethics and Public Management: Education and Training." Public Personnel Management 10, 1 (1981) 41-47.

This article suggests that the reality of administrative power, at macro and micro levels, combined with the variety of environmental values is the key to understanding and education for ethics in public administration. At the macro level the power of the bureaucracy has been a focus of attention in writing, Worthley suggests that bureaucrats must confront and be aware of the tremendous individual power that they have. He proposes a series of four training modules for ethics education.

179. Wulfemeyer, Kenneth Tim. Perceived Value of College Training by Professional Journalists in Three Metropolitan Areas. ED.D. Dissertation, University of California, Los Angeles (1981).

The value of a college education is being questioned today at least as much as at any other time in recent history. The value and content of college training for journalists has long been a subject of great controversy. The purpose of this study was to survey professional journalists to determine their perceived values of college training, the desirable knowledge, skills and personal characteristics necessary to become a successful journalist and recommended general education college courses and journalism courses.

A 45-question survey instrument was sent to 275 professional journalists at the major newspapers, radio stations and television stations in Des Moines, Iowa, San Diego, California and Honolulu, Hawaii. In order to enrich the survey data, personal interviews were conducted with 15 journalists.

Findings were based on 150 responses (55% return rate). Almost 90% of the respondents had at least a B.A. degree and over 67% had majored in journalism while in college. About 85% of the respondents were at least somewhat satisfied with their lives and 78% were satisfied with their jobs. Newspaper journalists were more satisfied with their jobs than were broadcast journalists.

About 76% of the respondents reported their jobs often allowed them to use their skills and knowledge fully. If a professional thought he was using his skills and knowledge fully, he was more likely to be satisfied with his job than a professional who thought he was not using his skills and knowledge fully.

The respondents recommended prospective journalists learn about governmental structures, liberal arts and sciences, English grammar, people, history, economics, current events, community structures, journalistic practices, laws, business, mathematics, writing styles and physical sciences. The respondents reported that a journalist should know how to write, deal with people, conduct research, edit, type, speak well, take notes, listen effectively and operate journalistic equipment.

The respondents listed a number of necessary personal characteristics journalists should have or develop. These included curiosity, persistence, reliability, patience, flexibility, aggressiveness, intelligence, ambition, friendliness, skepticism, common sense, enthusiasm and confidence.

About 87% of the respondents reported general college training was at least somewhat valuable for a person preparing for a career in journalism. Print journalists thought college training was more valuable than did broadcast journalists. The respondents recommended courses in political science, economics, history, English grammar, sociology, literature, business and psychology.

About 75% of the respondents reported college training in journalism was valuable for someone preparing for a career in journalism. Broadcast journalists and professionals who majored in journalism thought such training was more valuable than did newspaper journalists and professionals who did not major in journalism.

Recommended journalism courses included reporting, writing, law of mass communication, editing, internships with professional media, photography, ethics and history. About 9% of the respondents recommended prospective journalists take no college journalism courses.

Respondents were adamant about the importance of "practical, hands-on," experiential training in college for prospective journalists. About 82% of the respondents felt such training was valuable. Broadcast journalists thought practical training was more valuable than did newspaper journalists. Respondents also stressed the importance of some form of on-the-job training.

Finally, the respondents reported that their college experience had been valuable for providing general knowledge, improving clear thinking, providing leadership skills, providing a useful first-job skill, helping them to find a good job, providing currently used skills and knowledge, providing a necessary degree, helping to set life goals, helping them to achieve higher salaries, improving their lives and for helping to shape currently held attitudes, beliefs and values.

180. Zimmerman, Joseph F. "Ethics in the Public Service." State and Local Government Review 14, 3 (Spring 1982) 98-106.

Government actions to raise and maintain ethical standards in public service have resulted in the creation of conflict of interest laws, codes of ethics, financial disclosure acts, public meeting laws, freedom of information laws, and privacy acts. Codes of ethics deal with the most subtle ethical problems. Among the most difficult to control are violations of time rules, sick leave abuses, officials exceeding their legal authority, the revolving door problem between government and private industry, "whistle blowing," and abuse of citizen participation. To ensure that the standards of conduct in public service are raised, the codes need to be strengthened by removing or reducing opportunities for unethical behavior, including more rigorous screening of applicants and an adequate salary scale.

181. "A Code of Ethics: Excerpts from a Code Prepared by the Citizens Commission on Ethics in Government, Arlington County, VA." Public Administration Review 13, 2 (1953) 120-122.

A code prepared by the County Board of Arlington County, Virginia, "to help officials and citizens alike to come to a better judgment about what is right and what is wrong ethically in the exercise of public function.

182. "A Post-Watergate Code of Ethics." Public Management 57, 6 (June 1975) 7-12.

Two city managers and Elmer Staats, Comptroller General

of the U.S., as a panel, address such issues as the current
status of ethical conduct in the public service, the impact
of Watergate, and basic ethical problems faced by the local
professional city administrator.

183. "Guidelines and Standards for Professional Masters Degree
      Programs in Public Affairs/Public Administraion."
      Washington, D.C. National Association of Schools of
      Public Affairs and Administration (1974).

      Interesting for its emphasis on values as an important
      aspect in the education of administrators as well as a
      subsequent criteria upon which to evaluate the competence of
      these professionals.

184. "The Code of Ethics and Dual Officeholding Laws." Public
      Affairs Research Council of Louisiana, Inc. (November
      1979).

      A pamphlet clarifying both Louisiana's Codes of Ethics
      effective April 1, 1980, covering such areas as conflicts of
      interest, nepotism, influence peddling, financial disclosure
      and its Dual Officeholding Law (effective September 7,
      1979).

Chapter VII

Multiple Roles of Policy Analysts

185. Aberbach, Joel E., and Bert A. Rockman. "Clashing Beliefs
      Within the Executive Branch: The Nixon Administration
      Bureaucracy." American Political Science Review 70 (June
      1976) 456-468.

      Problems for the President in establishing control over
      policy within the executive agencies are examined
      empirically by surveying administrative officials to
      determine whether or not the basis for conflict rests with
      such characteristics as party affiliation, job status, views
      on social services, or agency affiliation. They conclude
      that agency and party affiliation are "particularly
      important in accounting for differences in views" among
      these officials.

186. Aram, John D. Dilemmas of Administrative Behavior.
      Englewood Cliffs, NJ: Prentice-Hall (1976).

      The author focuses on the fact that few dilemmas for
      administrators present themselves in a way which permits an
      easy choice for maximizing one criterion over another.
      Drawing on "writings in the fields of administration, social
      psychology, social and political theory, philosophy and
      fiction," Aram used real-world examples which emphasize
      opportunities for a "personal, existential decision."

187. Bailey, Stephen K. "Second Edition/Ethics and the
      Politician." The Center Magazine 5 (July 1968) 63-70.

      Based on the author's experiences as mayor of Middletown,
      Connecticut, the essay includes specific examples of ethical
      dilemmas which develop on a daily basis, illustrating his
      point that such problems seldom have an obvious solution.

188. Bernstein, Marver H. "Ethics in Government: The Problems
      in Perspective." National Civil Review 61 (July 1972)
      341-347.

      Current problems for State and local government personnel
      can be alleviated by providing "for clearer guidance in
      identifying major sources of unethical conduct...." Five
      steps toward better ethics in government should be adopted
      by State and local government personnel.

      Focusing specifically on state and local problems,
      Bernstein provides an overview of typical ethical issues
      confronting public officials. Solutions offered range from
      making legal officers available for advice and providing

orientation programs to granting authority to fire employees
not meeting ethical guidelines.

189. Boling, Edwin T., and John Dempsey. "Ethical Dilemmas in
      Government: Designing an Organizational Response."
      Public Personnel Management 10, 1 (1981) 11-19.

      The article focuses on the conceptual clarification as a
      building block to improve the ethical tenor of
      organizational life.

      This article focuses on the kinds of ethical problems
      that public administrators are likely to face. They
      include: (1) the ethics of public policy; (2) the personal
      ethical standards of administrators; and (3) organizational
      role demands. Ethics are identified as a major
      organizational component and three areas are suggested for
      reform in organizations. These are: (1) conceptual
      clarifications; (2) protection for dissenters; and (3)
      programs of normative enhancement. He argues that the most
      realistic solutions to the problems of morality and ethics
      may be in redesigning the organizational structures that
      constitute our public agencies.

190. Bolles, B. "Correctives for Dishonest and Unfair Public
      Administrators." Annals of the American Academy of
      Political and Social Science 363 (January 1966) 23-27.

      Bolles argues that dishonesty and unfairness are best
      corrected by forceful presidential leadership, attracting
      and retaining good people, internal accountability
      procedures, and immediate "retribution" when problems are
      discovered.

191. Bowie, Norman E., ed. Ethical Issues in Government.
      Philadelphia, PA: Temple University Press (1981).

      Contents are grouped under the headings: Should
      legislators serve constituents or conscience? The proper
      bounds of government regulation; The adequacy of
      cost-benefit analysis; The government's responsibility to
      inform the public.

      The decade of the seventies witnessed the rebirth of
      normative ethics. The focus of that rebirth seemed to be on
      professional ethics. Medical ethics led the way, but
      engineering ethics, nursing ethics, business ethics, and
      legal ethics have followed. This volume addresses some of

the issues that fall under the term "government ethics."
Specifically, it addresses the following questions: Should
legislators serve constituents or conscience? What are the
proper bounds of government regulation? Is cost-benefit
analysis an ethically acceptable tool for public policy
decisions? What is the government's obligation to inform
the public? Of course, these questions in no way exhaust
the list of questions that might properly be considered in a
volume on government ethics. Rather, they are meant to be
representative of the types of questions that arise in most
areas of applied ethics.

192. Braverman, Howard H. "Ethics Problems For Those Going In or
     Out of Some Public Offices." Illinois Bar Journal 71 98,
     2 (October 1982) 71.

193. Brownstein, Ronald. "Agency Ethics Officers Fear Meese
     Ruling Could Weaken Conflict Laws." National Journal 17
     (March 23, 1985) 639-642.

     This article reviews the actions relating to integration
     of ethics laws in the Reagan administration. David H.
     Martin, director of the office of government ethics wants to
     rewrite the federal conflict-of-interest-rules, contending
     that they are too vague. Martin sent a letter to Strom
     Thurmond in which he concluded that the requirement in the
     White House code to avoid appearances of impropriety was an
     ideal not a rigid rule. The article focuses on controversy
     of this decision.

194. Cleveland, Harlan. "A Philosophy for the Public Executive."
     Perspectives on Public Management: Cases and Learning
     Designs Robert T. Golembiewski (ed.) Itasca, Ill.: R.E.
     Peacock Pub. (1968).

     Cleveland believes that "public executives" can be
     identified as those whose attitudes reflect an awareness of
     and acceptance of their responsibility to the "public
     interest" rather than as those who are affiliated with
     public agencies. He calls for administrators who can accept
     the challenge demanded by the increasing "complexity" of
     public decision making.

195. Cleveland, Harlan, and Harold D. Laswell (eds). Ethics and
     Bigness: Scientific, Academic, Religious, Political and
     Military. New York: Harper and Brothers (1962).

     A collection of papers with comments by Wayne Leys,

Stephen Bailey, Paul Appleby, Eugene McCarthy, Talcott
Parsons and others examining the appropriate role for ethics
for administrators or executives faced with complex tasks
within a rapidly changing and pluralistic cultural milieu.

196. Cohen, William S. "Reforming the Special Prosecutor
      Process." American Bar Association Journal 68 (March
      1982) 278-281.

This article assesses the impact of the special
prosecutor provisions of the Ethics in Government Act of
1978 which required the appointment of a temporary
independent prosecutor to investigate alleged criminal
activities. The author argues that the act should be
amended to cover those situations that present the greatest
threat of conflict of interest fairness.

197. Cornog, Geoffrey Y. "Creating Moral Conditions in
      Organizations: The Challenge of Executive
      Responsibility." Public Administration Review 22, 2
      (Spring 1962) 98-103.

This essay weaves together the statements of scholars,
public figures, and executives regarding the need for ways
to achieve outstanding ethical behavior in organizations,
both public and private.

Cornog maintains that the problem of ethical behavior in
government is often mistakenly defined as the problem of
ethics in government, a formulation that leads to unsound
proposals for solving the problem. He defines the problem
as one of "ensuring that the actions of individuals conform
to some predetermined standard." The article also argues
that some ethical problems are created from the simultaneous
operation of several codes of conduct, which are at times
contradictory.

One proposed solution is to view public office as a
public trust, a trust that is dominant over any competing
demands. The article then examines two different methods
for achieving ethical behavior. The first is through
statute, administrative regulation and codes of ethics. The
second through the setting of high ethical standards by
leaders who provide personal examples of correct behavior,
and through increasing the quality of persons attracted to
public service.

198. Czajkoski, Eugene H. "A Brief For Public Policy Analysis in
      Criminological Research." Criminology 9 (August-November
      1971) 221-227.

      Radicalization pressures upon the social fabric are
      causing a revitalization of ethics and a strong humanist
      movement in the traditional academic disciplines.
      Considering criminology's laggardly appearance on the
      contemporary field of social policy conflict, criminology's
      development is retarded by its inattention to policy
      concerns. As our advancing Western civilization moves from
      one profound social crisis to another, there is a
      precipitous readiness to handle various kinds of social
      problems by defining undesirable or nonconforming behavior
      as criminal. The criminalization process provides a short
      circuit which cuts out the corrective ameliorative power of
      such established institutes as the family, the church and
      the school. The danger is that by looking to the criminal
      law to provide penalties for various minor forms of
      misconduct or nonconformity, the criminal law's
      effectiveness in dealing with more serious episodes of
      antisocial behavior is weakened. To prevent an artificial
      and disastrous polarization of our society, we need to
      practice some restraint in identifying what is criminal.
      This requires that criminologists attend to questions of
      public policy. Criminologists are now able to speak of
      normal crime and pathological crime. Normal crime is
      symptomatic of something wrong in the social structure and
      is therefore functional, ergo, normal. The proper response
      to normal crime (seen as a symptom) is to seek some
      reordering of the social nature of things. Pathological
      crime is seen as dysfunctional and the only response to it
      is to seek its extermination. Criminalization may be an end
      for various segments of the criminal justice system which
      derive assorted incomes from the management of criminality.
      Criminologists ought to be drawn from studying the product
      (the criminal) into studying the production system and the
      definitional process within it. By applying techniques of
      public policy analysis to the making and enforcing of
      criminal laws, the criminologist would bring an entirely
      different and much neglected perspective to the etiological
      study of crime. This different perspective would partially
      cast the criminologist in the role of an ethicist but would
      not bar him from using the tools of scientific inquiry.

199. Denhardt, Robert B. "Bureaucratic Socialization and
      Organizational Accommodation." Administrative Science
      Quarterly 13 (December 1968) 441-450.

A description of the mutual adjustments made by new employees and the existing organization of an Appalachian anti-poverty program as a result of conflicting socialization patterns.

This article examines the process of introducing bureaucratic organization to residents of Appalachia who were hired to work in a Community Action Program. Conflict between Appalachian culture and a bureaucratic mode of administration include a highly person-oriented culture vs. the impersonal office, and a suppression of authority vs. the hierarchical structure of the bureaucracy.

The organization also made adjustments to achieve compatibility with the local culture. The major change was to base supervision on a transactional form, which involved "bargaining among relative equals through a series of transactions." This mode organization was more congruent with the highly personalistic, egalitarian characteristics of the local workers.

200. Dvorin, Eugene P., and Robert H. Simmons. From Amoral to Humane Bureaucracy. San Francisco: Canfield Press (1972).

An essay challenging public administration to incorporate values into both its practice and its goals. A selected, annotated bibliography is provided.

This brief book raises a number of ethical issues useful for Public Policy and Administration. The manuscript will be useful for the student, practitioner, or layman concerned about the bureaucratic process. The analysis is based upon certain values about which the authors feel strongly. The book raises profound questions about the need for a humanistic bureaucracy.

201. Fishkin, James S. "Introduction to the Symposium: Theory and Practice of Representation." Ethics 91 (April 1981) 353-356.

Raises the issues of brainwashing and the implications of this for a democratic society.

The author states that if the brainwashing were sufficiently effective and pervasive, then the democratic machine would lack a necessary condition for any meaningful

claim to democracy--an (at least minimally) autonomous
citizenry. The forces of indoctrination would then be in
control of the machine. And a compelling claim to democracy
could not be sustained by reference to the design of the
machine itself--by any claims about the degree to which
power over the electoral results was equally shared among
the citizenry.

It is equally obvious that we might imagine a second kind
of society--one in which citizens formed their preferences
entirely free from any coercive influences that might be
characterized as brainwashing. These citizens might be
imagined as weighing (and publicly discussing) a wide
variety of alternatives with rational deliberation. And
only such preferences--"autonomously" arrived at--would be
fed into the democratic machine. If, however, the
democratic machine happened to be of standard
construction--not the ideal version imagined in our first
society--but one similar to those found in most electoral
systems around the world, it would have gross imperfections
and unequal weightings built into its very design. It could
fall far short of democratic aspirations as convincingly as
any variant of our first imaginary example above.

Clearly, then, we must distinguish two sets of issues:
(1) the design of the democratic machine itself and (2) the
character of the preferences fed into it. Democratic
aspirations for electoral systems must take account of the
degree of equality (both formal and substantive) under 1 and
the degree of autonomy under 2. Both sets of issues are,
however, complex and perplexing. The four long essays and
five brief comments which comprise this symposium attack
both sets of issues from a variety of directions.

202. Forester, John. "What Do Planning Analysts Do? Planning
      and Policy Analysis as Organizing." The Policy Studies
      Journal 9, 4 (February 1980-81) 595-604.

Analysts do more than solve problems and process
information. They organize others' attention to
possibilities for action and so shape expectations, working
relationships, participation, political support and
opposition, hopefulness, and resignation. A communicative
ethics that illuminates the practical choices planning
analysts routinely confront is indicated, covering questions
of whether to spread or withhold information, to raise or
lower expectations, to encourage and inform citizen action
and project reviews or to discourage them.

203. Foster, John L. "An Advocate Role Model for Policy
      Analysis." The Policy Studies Journal 8, 6 (June 1980)
      958-964.

      Emphasizing the fact that most approaches to policy
      evaluation, such as the problem solving models, or the new
      enlightenment model are most appropriate for the rather
      small number of policy issues that are clear-cut and well
      defined in nature. The author presents an advocacy approach
      intended to deal with more ambiguous issues and cases where
      multiple positions can co-exist. This model resembles the
      relationship between lawyer-client rather than the
      doctor-patient relationship of problem solving approaches.
      The policy evaluator's primary ethical consideration then
      becomes one of placing his/her clients' position or interest
      in an issue in the best light possible, short of outright
      fraud and/or data manipulation; instead of any quest for the
      truth. The author also discusses questions of feasibility,
      credibility, appropriate training, and ethics as they relate
      to the advocacy perspective.

204. Gallas, Geoffrey Scott. The Ethics, Politics and
      Administration of the American Judiciary: Toward a
      Substantive Perspective. D.P.A. Dissertation, University
      of Southern California (1977).

      At present, the field of judicial administration features
      an instrumental, operational or functional perspective.
      Proposed reforms inevitably yield paradoxical results. The
      assumption that national standards are applicable to all
      courts in every state, implying that differences in state
      and local political and administrative environments can be
      ignored, for example, is unlikely to lead to the achievement
      of even simple operational goals.

      Two key administrative reforms currently being advocated
      and undertaken in state court administration are examined in
      some detail: the unified court concept and judicial merit
      selection. The assumption underlying these reforms is that
      administrative fragmentation and disorganization are the key
      administrative issues. An alternative way of thinking about
      the organization of state court systems is outlined, one
      that is based on a more refined mode of instrumental
      thinking: contingency theory. Similarly, the judicial
      merit selection plan is deceptively simplistic with respect
      to factors affecting judicial quality, case of
      implementation, and long term consequences. The actual

power of selecting state judges is being shifted to a
central administrative staff. The viability of such
proposed administrative reforms, used largely on
administrative criteria, is questioned.

In this context it is argued that the conventional
field of judicial administration is unable to face squarely
either the necessity or the inevitability of political,
power-oriented judicial administrators. The analysis of the
tension between substance and methods is further articulated
in the organic connection of politics and administration.
It is argued that the difference between realpolitik and
efficiency on the one hand, and ethics and politics on the
other, should be clearly recognized.

205. Glazer, Myron. "Ten Whistleblowers and How They Fared."
      The Hastings Center Report 13, 6 (December 1983) 33-41.

An examination of the public disclosure of wrongdoing or
irresponsibility by employees in academic, industrial, and
governmental institutions. The following three distinct
paths of action are described: (1) unbending resisters
object within the organization to illegal or unethical
conduct they have seen; (2) implicated protestors speak out
within the organization, but acquiesce when threatened; and
(3) reluctant collaborators become deeply involved in
conduct they condemn privately and seek personal expiation
and public recourse only after they have left the
organization. Superiors respond to whistleblowers with
either punishment, ostracism, and silence, or support,
encouragement, and reinforcement. The cases of 10
whistleblowers are described.

206. Golembiewski, Robert T. "Organization as a Moral Problem."
      Public Administration Review 22, 2 (1962) 51-58.

Presents ways to organize work utilizing knowledge of
organizational behavior to accommodate ethics or values
"without sacrificing either efficiency or economy."

Organizational theory has focused on technical
considerations of what is related to what. This article
asserts that a second question must be asked. That question
is what relations are desirable and how are they to be
achieved. The first question is cited as implying an
empirical theory, while the second requires an ethical
orientation. The ethical orientation argues for a
value-driven set of prescriptions, based on the

Judeo-Christian tradition, to achieve desired relationships.

Traditional organization theory has four properties: (1) that authority should flow down from superiors to subordinates; (2) that supervision should be detailed and based on a narrow span of control; (3) that the organization of work should only consider the workers physical properties; and (4) that work should be routinized. The author lists five values for guiding organizational relations: (1) work must be psychologically acceptable and generally non-threatening; (2) work must allow the worker to develop their faculties; (3) the task must allow room for self-determination; (4) the worker must influence the work environment; and (5) the formal organization must not be the sole and final arbiter of behavior. Research evidence is then cited supporting the effectiveness of these values in organizations.

207. Maass, Arthur, and Laurence I. Radway. "Gauging Administrative Responsibility." Public Administration Review 9, 3 (1949) 182-193.

The authors develop criteria for judging the extent of responsibility by focusing on the purpose of responsibility--that is, "executing public policy," though the discussion implies policy making, as well--and the political forces deserving response. These forces include primarily the interest groups, the chief executive, the legislature, and less directly, political parties, professional affiliation, and citizens.

208. Mitcham, Carl, Paul Durbin, Albert Borgmann, Willis H. Truitt, and Edmund Byrne. "Scientists and Social Responsibility." Technology and Culture 18, 1 (January 1977) 56-61.

The University of Delaware's Science, Technology, and Society Committee in conjunction with the U's Values Center held a conference in July, 1975 to discuss the philosophy of technology. The historical antecedents for the philosophy of science, the philosopher's role in assessing technology, variety and types of technology, and technological responsibility to society were the major topics discussed. Carl Mitcham (St. Catherine College, KY) felt that the responsibility of technologists and technological philosophers was to provide a metaphysical approach to clarify how technology is based on other human creative efforts. Paul Durbin (University of Delaware, Newark) emphasized the necessity of scientists and technologists to become more concerned with politics and liberal causes, and adapt more Marxist techniques. Albert Borgmann (University of Montana, Missoula) suggested that technology should function to illustrate specific choices and courses of action for people, but not guide them. Willis H. Truitt (University of South Florida, Tampa) concurred with Durbin that science and technology cannot be isolated from other spheres, but stressed that there was not value neutrality in science and technology, just covert values and ethics. Edmund Byrne (Purdue University, Indianapolis, IN) proposed that technology, government, and citizens impress upon industry, issue and cause responsibility.

209. Murchie, David Neil. Morality and Social Ethics in the Thought of Charles Hodge. Ph.D. Dissertation, Drew University (1980).

This study offers an historical exposition of the social ethics of Charles Hodge, Princeton professor and renowned exponent of Old School Presbyterianism. Hodge's thought has generally been evaluated from the standpoint of his systematic theology; but his substantial interaction with the moral aspects of a wide range of political, economic, and social issues presents a dimension of Hodge's thinking that has been neglected by historians of American theology.

The dissertation initially considers the prominent background and methodological forces that influenced Hodge. Of major concern is the Scottish philosophy, particularly as expressed in the thought of Thomas Reid. Following the discussion of background and methodological influences, the study assesses the foundation elements underlying Hodge's ethical opinions. Following the discussion of foundational elements, the dissertation considers Hodge's attempts to apply biblical and theological criteria to specific issues.

The final evaluative discussion of Hodge's social ethics presents four thematic objectives present implicitly within Hodge's ethical writings which summarize his approach to the ethical task giving cohesion to the otherwise promiscuous arrangement of his ethical discussions.

210. Nader, Ralph, Peter J. Petkas, and Kate Blackwell (eds). Whistle Blowing: The Report of the Conference on Professional Responsibility. New York: Grossman Publishers (1972).

Declaring "the willingness and ability of insiders to blow the whistle is the last line of defense ordinary citizens have against the denial of their rights and the destruction of their interests by secretive and powerful institutions," Ralph Nader sets tone for this report combining major addresses to the Conference, testimony by and about whistle blowers, suggestions for change in major types of institutions to encourage openness, and strategies for those who believe they must blow the whistle.

211. Peters, Charles, and Taylor Branch (eds). Blowing the Whistle: Dissent in the Public Interest. New York: Praeger Publishers (1972).

A collection of essays arguing that "whistle blowing is part of a movement toward conscience by employee...." They call for providing more protection for the whistle blower while, at the same time, not providing sanctions for "free riders" or those seeking to keep jobs by directing focus toward others instead of himself/herself.

212. Plant, Jeremy F., and Harold F. Gortner. "Ethics, Personnel Management, and Civil Service Reform." Public Personnel Management 10, 1 (1981) 3-10.

Despite a variety of suggested approaches to the study of ethics in the public service, and popular and scholarly interest in the issues of government ethics since the 1970's, ethics in government remains a subject that seems incapable of resolution or definitional clarity. In spite of the efforts of scholars and practitioners to grapple with the meaning of ethics in the public service, the issue remains an area of public administration that appears unable to be managed. That is, it has been difficult to (1) define the problem, (2) set objectives, (3) create programs specifically aimed toward goal achievement, and (4) establish clearcut evaluative standards by which the attainment of objectives can be measured and their impacts judged.

While all managers have been challenged by the problem of finding ways to improve ethical conduct in government, personnel executives have played a major role in this ongoing drama. At least four factors have created this role for personnel administrators. First, the civil service system, with its emphasis on merit principles, was created in a burst of moral outrage which presented personnel reform (during the late 1800's and early 1900's) as a path to "good government." Second, personnelists have always had the responsibility of focusing their attention on individuals in positions--with all of the concomitant regard for the skills, responsibilities, and pressures of the job--rather than facing the pressure of program management with its emphasis on goals and achievement of productivity levels. Third, the functions of training, correction of hiring and promotion inequities, and handling disciplinary actions against employees who violated canons of ethical conduct (until 1978) have forced personnelists to play an active role in specific applications of rules to ethical problems. Finally, until recently, personnel administrators functioned in the role of counselor to incumbent public officials coping with difficult situations involving ethical choices. These issues are addressed in this article.

213.   Riggs, Fred W. "Three Dubious Hypotheses: A Comment on Heper, Kin, and Pai." Administration and Society 12, 3 (November 1980) 301-326.

This article presents a critical assessment of a recent study by Heper, Kim, and Pei (1980) on the role of bureaucrats and regime types on public administration in South Korea and Turkey. After presenting the historical background to the study of comparative public administration, the writer concentrates on the substantive aspects of the study, centering on its three major hypotheses regarding: 1) The role of the bureaucracy in decisionmaking; 2) Bureaucratic accountability; 3) The relationship between professional norms and regime type. These hypotheses are found to be based on incorrect interpretations of the literature. In this way, the non-confirmation of the study's hypotheses does not disprove previous findings in the area, as the researchers claim. Instead, it demonstrates the need for more accuracy in reading the research literature. Even so, the study does generate useful new data, and confirms the importance of regime type as a factor influencing bureaucratic behavior.

214.   Rogowski, Ronald. "Representation in Political Theory and in Law. (Symposium: Theory and Practice of Representation)." Ethics 91, 3 (April 1981) 395-430.

This article treats three aspects of the problem of representation. "First, he tries to discover what, basically, is meant by "representation" or "being represented," and thus to order and make sensible the apparent variety of meanings exhibited by Beer, Pitkin, and

others. Finally, he suggests how the first two sets of
results may help to resolve some of the difficulties in
recent American legislation and jurisprudence about
representation, including particularly the problems of
legislative districting and apportionment. In each case, he
tries to show how some of the concepts of formal theory can
lend clarity and precision; but he is aware that he is neither
a mathematician nor a lawyer and that these efforts are
therefore perilous.

215. Rohr, John A. "Financial Disclosure: Power in Search of
      Policy." Public Personnel Management 10, 1 (1981) 29-40.

The purpose of this article is to attempt to contribute
to the public argument over financial disclosure (FD) so
that it can achieve its goal of detecting and deterring
conflicts of interest without needlessly compromising the
privacy of public officials. At the outset it must be
acknowledged that the view presented here is that of a
friendly critic of much of the current discussion in support
of FD. This attitude will be criticized in a way that
hopefully will be of interest to those who are affected by
such laws as well as to those who formulate them.

The article's subtitle, "Power in Search of Policy,"
suggests that the connection between specific provisions of
FD laws and the purpose of such laws is not always as clear
as the constitutional power of federal, state, and local
governments to compel FD. Presumably, the primary purpose
of compelling FD is to detect and deter conflicts of
interest. It is the relationship between this commendable
goal and specific FD mandates that is at times quite
obscure. A telling symptom of this problem is the fact that
the federal "Ethics in Government Act of 1978," though in
many ways a sound and sensible statute, has neither a
preamble nor a statement of legislative intent.

Whatever the problems one might raise over the ends and
means of FD, the power of the several levels of government
to enact FD presents few serious difficulties. When the
recent federal act was working its way through Congress, the
House Select Committee on Ethics dismissed any
constitutional scruples over compelling disclosure by simply
calling attention to "the overwhelming state court and
Supreme Court precedents upholding financial disclosure
laws."

216. Rose-Ackerman, Susan. Corruption: A Study in Political
     Economy. New York: Academic Press (1978).

Both economists and political scientists have, each in
their own ways, harbored strangely idealized views of the
modern state. The blind spots in each field arise in part
from an imperfect understanding of the neighboring
discipline. On the one hand, economists have often left the
analysis of governmental structures to political scientists,
contenting themselves with a study of the costs and benefits
of substantive policy alternatives. On the other hand,
political scientists have viewed the competitive
relationship among political actors in a way which
economists would find simplistic.

The main aim of this book has been to demonstrate that
each of these analytic strands, and their
interrelationships, must be specified clearly if we are to
grasp the corrupt incentives inherent in a given political
structure. Thus, in examining the relationship between
governmental institutions and corruption, analysts must move
beyond crude contrasts between autocratic regimes and the
more decentralized and democratic types that are the major
concern of this study. The author has shown that the
opportunities for corruption remain high if bureaucrats and
legislators can collude on a common strategy, despite an
institutionalized system of checks and balances. Her major
purpose has been to examine the pathology of relatively
healthy organisms, thus she has concentrated upon political
systems in which legislative-bureaucratic collusion is not a
central problem.

217. Spiro, Herbert J. Responsibility in Government: Theory and
     Practice. New York: Van Nostrand (1969).

An in-depth study of "responsibility" as a fundamental
element in a "constitution democracy" in which citizens must
assume political responsibility. Spiro argues that the
administrator must be concerned with the challenge of
preserving the constitutional democracy with "success as a
by-product" rather than the primary goal—that individuals
need opportunities to develop and exercise their
responsibilities as citizens more than they need to
experience efficiency.

218. Studer, Kenneth E., and Daryl E. Chubin. "Ethics and the
     Unintended Consequences of Social Research: A
     Perspective from the Sociology of Science." Policy

Sciences 8, 2, (June 1977) 111-124.

It is argued that "successful" social science requires
the development of a social ethic or sense of research
responsibility. An examination of impediments to ethical
reflection in sociology suggests that an individualistic
orientation is ineffective in coping with the unintended
consequences of social research. Such consequences can be
particularly harmful in the sociology of science where
policy research and governmental support for its production
often entail an "indiscriminate advocacy of knowledge."
Such advocacy raises anew questions of the power of
scientific knowledge, the definition of client-professional
relationships, and the collection of data that may not only
violate the intent of individuals and groups supplying
information, but may undermine the credibility of sociology
itself.

219. Thompson, Dennis. "Ascribing Responsibility to Advisers in
      Government." Ethics 93, 3 (April 1983) 546-560.

The article criticizes the three theoretical claims that
are used to absolve governmental advisors of responsibility
for their acts. These include: 1) The causal criterion
that the advisee, as a free agent, breaks the causal drain
by his decision; 2) The limiting of responsibility only to
those results intended by the advisor; and 3) The
limitations of the advisor's role. Thompson finds none of
these adequate, but suggests that together they reveal some
criteria for evaluating an advisor's responsibility.

220. Waldo, Dwight. "Reflections on Public Morality."
      Administration and Society 6 (November 1974) 267-282.

Stating that "governmental action does not lend itself to
moral absolutes and is not to be judged by them," Waldo
suggests that the origins of and transitions in public
morality demonstrate that moral problems for governmental
action will only become more complex in the future. He
offers the literature in seven substantive areas from which
ideas may be gleaned to deal with the increasing confusion
over public morality: "utopias"; feudalism; "stateless
societies"; pluralism; "one world"; "democratic" vs.
bureaucratic administration; and "organizational
citizenship."

221. "Professional Ethics in Government Side-Switching." Harvard
      Law Review 96 (June 1983) 1914-1930.

      This article argues that when the government switches
      sides, the government attorneys who were previously involved
      in the case should be disqualified. First, the article
      argues that although government side-switching may be an
      acceptable practice, government attorneys involved in
      side-switching are not free of ethical obligations to
      cooperating parties. The article then explored methods that
      should be used by the courts to enforce these obligations.

      This concern grew out of an effort to overturn a state
      law that prevented the school district from implementing a
      voluntary school busing program. The Reagan administration
      changed the policy on busing.

222. "Serving Two Masters: A Common Cause Study of Conflicts of
      Interest in the Executive Branch." Common Cause (1976).

      This study uses empirical data to document its findings
      that "potential conflict of interest and the possibility of
      serious agency bias (exists), throughout the executive
      bureaucracy." Suggested reform measures include requiring
      top officials to file financial disclosure statements,
      divest themselves of financial interests which pose a
      possible conflict of interest, restrict their
      post-employment opportunities, and increase review and
      enforcement of these existing regulations.

Chapter VIII

Criteria for the Analysis of Alternatives and
Principles of Decision-Making

223. Anderson, Charles W. "The Place of Principles in Policy
     Analysis." American Political Science Review 73
     (September 1979) 711-723.

     Any theory of policy evaluation has to address the
     problem of the choice of criteria for decision making. In
     most theories of policy rationality, derived from economic
     theories of the utility-maximizing individual and a
     positivist conception of valuation, such values are to be
     regarded as the "preferences" of the policy maker. The
     stipulation and ordering of standards of judgment is not
     considered to be part of policy rationality itself. This
     conception of rationality is not obligatory. Understanding
     rationality as having good reasons for an action, and policy
     judgment as a process of argument, enables us to stipulate
     certain standards at the metapolitical level which any
     system of policy evaluation must meet. It is possible to
     identify a logical sense in which such classic principles as
     authority, justice and efficiency can be understood as
     necessary considerations in any rationally defensible policy
     appraisal.

224. Blumberg, Stephen K. "Notes on the Art of Administration."
     Midwest Review of Public Administration 14, 3 (September
     1980) 191-199.

     Luther Gulick in 1936 created the acronym "POSDCORB" to
     describe the duties of an administrator: 1) Planning; 2)
     Organizing; 3) Staffing; 4) Directing; 5) Coordinating;
     6) Reporting; and 7) Budgeting. These dictates cover the
     technical aspects of administration adequately; however,
     needed humanistic guidelines are not included. Such
     guidelines are described here, using the acronym
     "EVPOSDCORB": 1) Ethics; 2) Values; 3) Patience; 4)
     Openness; 5) Sensitivity; 6) Dignity; 7) Cooperation; 8)
     Responsiveness; and 9) Beneficence. An awareness of the
     dictates within both acronyms is necessary for effective
     management.

225. Bowman, James S. "Ethics in the Federal Service: A
     Post-Watergate View." Midwest Review of Public
     Administration 11, 1 (March 1977) 3-20.

     The author surveys the attitudes of public managers
     employed by the federal government to see how they perceive
     the state of ethical concern in the government today and the
     role of ethics in the operations of public agencies. The
     federal executives were questioned in 1975-1976. These

administrators had a high degree of concern about the
ethical dimensions of American government and public policy
issues. Findings on more specific ethical problems and
issues are then explained: 1) Thirty percent of the
executives believe that ethics today are superior to those
of earlier periods; 2) Executives feel pressure to
compromise their standards to achieve organizational goals;
3) Almost one-half feel that the illegal uses of the
Central Intelligence Agency and the Federal Bureau of
Investigation are realistic examples of the ethics in
contemporary politics. There is also a discussion of the
executives' attitudes on the ethics in the daily operations
of government. The findings here indicate that these
executives believe that they are more ethical than their
peers and their superiors. Several implications of these
findings are presented (e.g., the fact that even the most
repugnant activities are acceptable to some suggests that
everyone has an individual set of standards that can be
adjusted to various types of situations). Several
conclusions are discussed (e.g., superiors can play a
significant role in upgrading ethical conduct, a renewed
emphasis on professional conduct offers the opportunity for
conscientious public servants to clarify behavior and to
make codes and regulations effective).

Bowman surveyed the attitudes toward ethics of a sample
of federally employed public administrators. While
concluding that, overall, participants demonstrated a high
degree of concern over both macro (government-wide) level
and micro (agency) level ethics, Bowman believes that "some
kind of institutional basis for professional conduct is
necessary."

226. Bowman, James S. "Ethical Issues for the Public Manager."
      In William B. Eddy (ed). Handbook on Public
      Organizational Management. New York: Marell Dekker,
      Inc. 1983.

Managers must be able to identify ethical issues and
articulate thoughtful responses. This article provides an
understanding of many of the conceptual, individual,
organizational, and administrative issues surrounding ethics
in government. The article is exploratory in nature,
providing basic tools, background information, and critical
standards to approach and evaluate ethical questions in
public service.

227. Brooks, Harvey. "Technology and Values: New Ethical Issues
     Raised by Technological Progress." Zygon, Journal of
     Religion and Science 8 (March 1973) 17-35.

     Brooks believes that values are culturally based. In
     addition, those values which are transmitted to succeeding
     generations are those which enhance survival. He expresses
     concern for the decisions which we are delaying for future
     generations such as nuclear waste storage and continuing
     presence of low-level toxics in the environment.

228. Chitwood, Stephen R. "Social Equity and Social Service
     Productivity." Public Administration Review 34, 1
     (January-February 1974) 29-35.

     Attempts to establish a conceptual base for further
     discussion and research incorporating "social equity" as
     part of the standard for measuring productivity in the
     distribution of government services.

     Chitwood acknowledges the importance of measuring
     productivity (the relationship of outputs to inputs) in
     public service, but maintains that the social equity in the
     distribution of public goods and services is often neglected
     by measures which focus on the quantity of services. He
     classifies the dimensions of social equity as: (1) equal
     services to all; (2) proportionally equal services to all;
     and (3) unequal services to individuals based on relevant
     differences, and states that the social equity with which
     public goods and services are distributed will become
     increasingly important.

229. Cleveland, Harlan. "How Do You Get Everybody in on the Act
     and Still Get Some Action?" Public Management 57, 6
     (June 1975) 3-6.

     A reprint of a lecture delivered during the 1974 annual
     meeting of ASPA in Syracuse advocating a middle-road between
     openness and secrecy in government. While acknowledging the
     importance of openness, Cleveland cautions that "the paradox
     of participation" is that too much of it makes for
     polarization and "mediocre" decisions rather than bold and
     innovative ideas.

230. Crosby, Michael. "Selling Cigarettes to the Third World."
     Christianity and Crisis 43 (May 30, 1983) 212-215.

     Crosby reviews the health and social costs of smoking,

and questions the ethics of exports to third world countries. The article also describes company reactions to shareholder proposals about such exports at shareholder meetings of the Philip Morris and R.J. Reynolds tobacco companies.

231. Deigh, John. "And Justice for All: New Introductory Essays in Ethics and Public Policy." (book reviews) Ethics 94, 178 (October 1983).

This is a review of a collection of twelve essays written by philosophers. It consists of seven essays on topics of public interest, five of which address general topics in ethics and social theory. Deigh states that the level of depth and required level of philosophical background is uneven, and suggests that it be carefully examined before adopting it for a course text.

232. Deknatel, Charles Y. "Questions About Environmental Ethics -- Toward a Research Agenda with a Focus on Public Policy." Environmental Ethics 2, 4 (Winter 1980) 353-362.

Identified are common elements in environmental ethics, e.g.: (1) moral criteria involving humans with regard to nature, (2) a long-term perspective adjunct to biological dynamics, and (3) an assessment of natural resources that emphasized intrinsic, noneconomic values. However, the application of these elements to related policy or action is not always clear. Developed are questions and a preliminary framework for considering issues raised by environmental ethics as they could appear in public policy. Criteria for measuring the content and level of responsibility of environmental ethics are discussed, as is their role and function.

233. Diesing, Paul. "Noneconomic Decision-Making." Ethics 66, 1 (October 1955) 18-35.

Provides "an alternative method of decision-making purposely centered on noneconomic factors of social life" rather than on "maximizing utility" by introducing the importance of such concepts as integration, creativity, and growth as part of the decision process.

234. Elliston, Frederick, and Norman Bowie, eds. A Review of "Ethics, Public Policy, and Criminal Justice."

This is a detailed review of this book. It is divided
into five parts. Part I (4 chapters) is entitled the
Concept of Crime. Part II (5 chapters) addresses five
separate moral issues in criminal justice. Part III (6
chapters) discusses ethical issues in the apprehension,
trials, and sentencing of criminals. Part IV (4 chapters)
looks at the consequences of sentencing decisions. Part V
(4 chapters) is described as serving as the cap to the book
and includes essays on public policy and crime, impediments
to rational criminal justice planning, ethical issues in
teaching criminal justice and a theory of criminological
ethics. Felkenes states that this book, or one like it,
should be required in the criminal justice curriculum,
adding that the selection of the essays is excellent.

235. Felkenes, George T. A Review of "Ethics, Public Policy, and
      Criminal Justice." Edited by Frederick Elliston and
      Norman Bowie. Oegeschlager, Gunn, Hain Publishers, Inc.
      Reviewed in Journal of Criminal Justice 12 (July-August
      1984) 421-425.

The study of ethics and moral issues by practitioners,
students, and scholars in criminal justice has been
haphazard at best and nonexistent at worst. There does
appear to be in today's academic inquiry into the
complexities of the criminal justice system a flickering
interest in ethical and moral problems that impact ever
increasingly on the people who make up the system
functionaries and how the system operates in a democratic
society.

This volume, edited by Frederick Elliston and Norman
Bowie, is a collection of essays that covers systematically
and representatively the entire gamut of moral issues facing
persons in the system and academic scholars in criminal
justice.

Study of ethics and philosophy conjures up new visions of
justice that can serve to direct and shape the actions of
criminological theorists, criminal justice functionaries,
criminal justice students, and criminal justice scholars.
For this general purpose, an awareness of the moral issues
involved in criminal justice, the Ellison and Bowie
compilation of scholarly papers is a very welcome addition
to criminal justice and criminology literature.

236. Fischer, Frank. "Ethical Discourse in Public
      Administration." Administration and Society 15, 1 (May

1983) 5-42.

The article presents an argument for ethics and normative discourse and rhetoric in public policy making and public administration, including a framework for a model developed from the article's central theme of the informal logic of practical reason. Posited as a guide to decision-making, the framework is a logic of questions systematically integrating empirical and normative judgments. It proceeds on four levels, each with its own specific logic and purpose: 1) verification; 2) validation; 3) vindication; and 4) rational choice. The first two constitute first-order discourse concerned with reasoning within a specific value system, the second two, second order discourse questioning the value system itself.

237. Fishkin, James. "Moral Principles and Public Policy." Daedalus 108, 4 (Fall 1979) 55-67.

Although morality has always been present in public policy debates, scholars during the first half of the twentieth century tended to adopt a neutral position on moral issues. Political theory itself seemed dead. Yet the upheavals of the sixties, including the Vietnam War and the civil rights battle, brought moral questions back into the realm of public policy. The author believes, however, that the ethical criteria being applied to public policy are not adequate because they fail a test he has devised: they support policy that imposes severe deprivation on some segment of the population whereas alternative policies would not have done so. Three types of principles exist: procedural, structural, and absolute-rights. They are examined with respect to this test, and all are found to be lacking. The author concludes that new principles must be developed that will better deal with the ethics of public policy.

238. Foster, Gregory D. "Legalism, Moralism and the Bureaucratic Mentality." Public Personnel Management 10, 1 (1981) 93-97.

The government of the future can be expected to assume added responsibility for coping with an uncertain environment. This will demand creative public servants to resolve fundamental value conflicts. Unfortunately, most administrators manifest a form of legalistic or "grooved" thinking that reflects an entrenched acculturation process. If civil servants are to perform effectively in the future,

they must be imbued with a moralistic outlook that enables
them to make responsible decisions in the face of an
increasingly demanding environment.

239. Freed, Clifford. "Ethical Considerations for the Justice
Department When it Switches Sides During Litigation."
University of Puget Sound Law Review 7 (Winter 1984)
405-424.

This article discusses the changing of sides by the
Justice Department in the Supreme Court case of Washington
vs. Seattle School District No. 1. The sole reason for the
change is cited as the change of administrations during the
case. The article goes on to state that the ABA Code of
Ethics rarely addresses government attorneys, and that while
the switch did not clearly deviate from the Code, the
reversal violated the spirit of the Code. Freed then
selects relevant canons of the ABA Code of Ethics and
analyzes the actions of the Justice Department in the light
of these canons. He concludes that the betrayal of the
coparties in the suit erodes confidence in the
administration of justice, and that in like cases the
department should be forced to withdraw from the case.

240. Gawthrop, Louis C. "Administrative Responsibility: Public
Policy and the Wilsonian Legacy." Policy Studies Journal
5, 1 (Autumn 1976) 108-113.

For Woodrow Wilson and other early twentieth century
public administrators, the issue concerning administrative
responsibility was lack of operating techniques rather than
the ethical-moral vacuousness that is of concern now. Until
notions of ethical responsibility extend beyond a mere
mechanical adherence to the explicit letter of the law, the
study of public administration must continue to reflect the
Wilsonian emphasis on operating techniques. The "ethics of
civility" are based on a common-sense, day-to-day relevance
of political efficacy without reference to moral tenets. A
redefinition of administrative responsibility is needed,
based more on individual integrity. However, the notion of
administrative responsibility is much too important to be
left to each individual to define. It must combine the
elements of both the collective disparate design and the
individual morality. In conjunction with an explicitly
avowed ethics of consciousness, a new openness of
administrative responsibility would be gained. An ethics of
consciousness may provide an authentic public
responsibility.

The author analyzes the nature of administrative responsibility in U.S. public agencies. At present, the study of administrative responsibility reflects an emphasis on operating techniques. This emphasis is attributed to Woodrow Wilson and other early 20th century students of public administration. In criticizing this mechanical focus of administrative responsibility, the author claims that ethical perceptions of administrative responsibility must be considered, at the very least, quaint. He states that until public administrators are prepared to go beyond a mere mechanical adherence to the letter of the law, the study of public administration will continue to reflect the Wilsonian emphasis on operating techniques. The author introduces the concept of an ethics of civility (an ethic based on a common-sense, day-to-day relevance of political efficacy, without consideration of moral tenets), and contends that this is at the basis of the present conception of administrative responsibility. As a counterpart to the ethics of civility, the author presents what he calls an ethics of consciousness (an ethic based on the individual conscience). Its development has been muted in the present administrative environment, which is sensitized solely to the notion of not doing that which should not be done. The argument is presented for a new administrative ethic based on the ethics of consciousness. Some implications of administrative responsibility based on each type of ethic are explained.

241. Godfrey, Jr., E. Drexel, and Elliot Zashin. "Integrity in Work and Interpersonal Relations: A Perspective for the Public Manager." Public Personnel Management 10, 1 (1981).

Much of the concern for ethics in government has focused on decisions and behaviors that violated constitutional norms, rules of the political game, on conventional morality. For the average civil servant, however, ethical issues are likely to arise from much more mundane activities. The authors argue that the actions (or inactions) of managers in dealing with work norms and interpersonal relationships can have a very significant impact on the ethical quality of the work environment. Several kinds of situations are described, criteria for evaluating an administrator's handling of ethical issues are proposed, and recommendations for creating an open atmosphere are explored.

242. Grofman, Bernard. "Fair and Equal Representation."
     (Symposium: Theory and Practice of Representation)
     Ethics 91, 3 (April 1981) 477-485.

     This article is included in a symposium on ethics
     sponsored by the National Science Foundation. Grofman
     provides a critical response to formal papers presented at
     the University of Chicago. The author raises an issue in
     this paper which is related to political equality. He
     states that equality is not a single concept but a group of
     distinct, but related criteria.

243. Hart, David K. "Social Equity, Justice and the Equitable
     Administrator." Public Administration Review 34, 1
     (January-February 1974) 3-11.

     The author argues in favor of "public administration
     philosophers" trained in ethics so that they can develop a
     "rigorous... theory of social equity" based on John Rawls'
     principles of justice as developed in his A Theory of
     Justice and the lessons of "applied public administration."

     Hart argues for a public administration ethic based on
     the theory of justice developed by John Rawls. This ethic
     would give the social equity concerns of the "New Public
     Administration" a central position in the conduct of public
     administration. After a cursory examination of Rawls'
     theory, Hart presents five arguments for a public
     administration based on social equity.

244. Howe, Elizabeth, and Jerome Kaufman. "Ethics and
     Professional Practice in Planning and Related Policy
     Professions." Policy Studies Journal 9, 4, Special #2
     (1980-81) 585-595.

     This article explores the ethical attitudes of urban
     planners. The authors state that ethics are related to
     either ends, the goals of professionals, or to means, or the
     way in which professionals might work to achieve the ends.
     The authors surveyed members of the American Institute of
     Planners, presenting them with scenarios and questions about
     whether certain behaviors were ethical. The results are
     reported and the authors conclude that the study provides
     insight into the ethical perceptions of the sample and
     reveals inconsistencies between accepted professional ethics
     and the planner's perceptions of ethics.

245. Leys, Wayne A.R. Ethics for Policy Decision: The Art of
      Asking Deliberative Questions. New York: Prentice-Hall
      (1952).

      After reviewing the major systems of ethics (such as
      those from Bentham, Socrates and Plato, Kant, etc.), Leys
      uses actual policy choices made in the past, for example,
      TVA, to demonstrate for the reader how the questions posed
      by philosophers can be combined with the practitioner's
      recognition of important considerations in each case to
      provide insight for the decision maker and improve the
      ethical quality of his judgments.

246. Lilla, Mark T. "Ethos, 'Ethics' and Public Services."
      Public Interest 63 (Spring 1981) 3-17.

      A review of the history of teaching public administration
      reveals that the rise of "public policy" instruction led to
      the dissolution of a widely shared democratic ethos of
      administration. This ethos has been replaced by teaching in
      "ethics," which is neither proper moral philosophy nor
      effective moral education. It is argued that this ethos
      must be revived if United States schools of public policy
      are to produce public officials with moral habits rather
      than specious "ethical" casuistry.

      While college enrollments are declining, new programs on
      ethics and government are proliferating. Many public
      officials are being schooled in the fields of public policy
      and public administration and are learning the art of
      ethical discourse without its necessary corollary, moral
      education. This results in the training of casuists rather
      than truly moral public servants. Applied ethics focuses on
      analysis rather than moral reasoning and acquisition of
      moral habits. The moral education of public servants can
      best be done by sensitive teachers who can transmit an ethos
      to students, not by teachers trained in contemporary
      philosophical ethics.

      At the end of the nineteenth century, the public
      administration profession was developed; academic programs
      in the field were started in the early 1900s. A strong
      sense of ethos was transferred from teachers to students.
      Governmental and academic changes in the 1960s caused a
      shift. The field was known as public policy and the main
      emphasis was on analytic techniques. The infusion of ethos
      was absent; by the 1970s the need for moralistic learning
      introduced new moral-political philosophers to the core of

the discipline. This new form of applied ethics is seen as a kind of casuistry. Students of the field, though they have the training to analyze situations from an ethical standpoint, lack the ingrained morality which results from acquisition of the attitudes and habits of the administrative ethos.

247. Lineberry, Robert L., and Robert E. Welch, Jr. "Who Gets What: Measuring the Distribution of Urban Services." Social Science Quarterly 54 (March 1974) 700-712.

Recent urban policy research has been focused on the determinants of local policy outputs, concentrating on the effects of social economic and political factors on governmental outputs. The results of these studies is described as showing that economic resources account for most of the variation in per capita expenditure levels. The authors suggest that researchers should direct their attention to the distribution of costs, benefits, and sanctions.

The distributional question was framed by Lasswell as "who gets what, when, how." Lineberry and Welch assert that today's cities are service-dependent environments, that the distributional question relates to some major social problems (inadequate police, education and other services are cited as grievances causing urban disturbances), and that the distribution of services has been the focus of a legal campaign which maintains that disparities in the distribution of services may violate the equal protection clause of the fourteenth amendment.

The remainder of the article outlines the difficulties of measuring and collecting systematic evidence on the distribution of urban services, and offers suggestions on how to resolve these difficulties.

248. Loucks, Edward A. "Bureaucratic Ethics from Washington to Carter: An Historical Perspective." Public Personnel Management 10, 1 (1981) 77-82.

The developmental phases of American ethical history are the topic of this article. Loucks claims that Judeo-Christian thought, particularly the Golden Rule, is an appropriate starting point for the discussion and goes on to state that the phases in this ethical history are distinguished by whether the Golden Rule was internalized by practitioners, or imposed on them by an external "coercive" force. The phases are cited as (1) the era of George Washington (1798-1828), (2) Andrew Jackson and the Career Bureaucrat (1828-1883), (3) Woodrow Wilson and the Birth of the Civil Service (1883-1937), and (4) the New Deal Bureaucrat (1937-1978).

249. Lovrich, Jr., Nicholas P. "Professional Ethics and the Public Interest: Sources of Judgment." Public Personnel Management 10, 1 (1981) 87-92.

This paper discusses the proper understanding of the character of professionalism and personal ethics in public service. The author is concerned with an individual's conception of the public interest as it relates to ethical conduct and civil service. In addition an attempt is made to develop a framework for the consideration of the major contending perspectives on the public interest. The presence of contending views of the public interest can provide a useful comparison of perspectives on public interest for students and practitioners.

250. Marini, Frank (ed). Toward a New Public Administration: the Minnowbrook Perspective. Scranton, PA.: Chandler Publishing Co. (1971).

A collection of the papers presented at the Minnowbrook Conference with comments and editorial notes throughout. Marini identifies some of the themes from the conference as: "relevance, antipositivism, personal morality, innovation, concern for clients, antibureaucratic philosophy." George Frederickson uses the following "subtopics: dissatisfaction with the state of the disciplines; moral, ethics, and values; social equity; client-focus; and repression." Although the entire collection is worth examining, selected articles have indexed separately.

251. Nelson, A. D. "Ethical Relativism and the Study of Political Values." Canadian Journal of Political Science 11 (1978) 3-31.

Though not specifically concerned with public administration, this piece examines the question of "why" versus "why not" study values concluding that their common use by everyone in decision making makes them intuitively interesting.

252. Porter, David O., and Teddie Wood Porter. "Social Equity and Fiscal Federalism." Public Administration Review 34, 1 (January-February 1974) 36-43.

Explores the implications of social equity for the distribution of income and opportunities in the United States and calls for major reforms in the existing distribution framework in order to achieve a "more equitable and integrated system of fiscal federalism."

253. Poston, Ersa, and Walter D. Broadway (eds). "Ethics and Morality in Government: Public Policy Forum." The Bureaucrat 4 (April 1975).

This forum was planned to help the reader understand the forces affecting ethics in government from three perspectives: 1) how an individual actually identifies ethical dilemmas; 2) what training and education is best for public servants, and 3) how the social and organizational context can affect decision making. Individual articles are listed separately by author's name.

254. Rizzo, Ann-Marie, and Thomas J. Patka. "The Organizational Imperative and Supervisory Control: Their Effects on Managerial Ethics." Public Personnel Management 10, 1 (1981).

This article reports a study which explored supervisory input into ethical dilemmas faced by their subordinate managers. The study used hypothetical scenarios. The following hypotheses were tested with the results following hypothesis: (1) supervisory control would vary directly with organizational significance--supported, (2) support for subordinate ethics would vary inversely with organizational significance--supported, and (3) hypotheses three and four tested independence of supervisory control, support for subordinate ethics and organizational significance. The results for these were reported as being less clear.

The authors suggest that pragmatism is highly valued in organizations and that knowing what is ethical may be less of a problem than acting on that knowledge.

255. Roth, Guenther. "Max Weber's Ethics and the Peace Movement Today." Theory and Society 13, 4 (July 1984) 491-511.

Max Weber's concept of "responsibility before history," enunciated at the turn of the century, and his notions of

the ethics of "conviction" and "responsibility" are
transposed to the contemporary West German setting and used
to assess the positions of the peace movement and the
government with respect to the issue of nuclear arms.
Weber's ethic of responsibility is used by government
officials to justify their refusal to expel nuclear weapons.
However, the new ethical situation renders the survival of
entire populations, not just that of specific nation-states,
questionable in the case of nuclear war. Thus, the ethic of
conviction, i.e., the inner sense of the gross immorality of
decisions leading to nuclear annihilation, even if contrary
to "national interest," should be the dominant criterion.

256. Sagoff, Mark. "Do We Need a Land Use Ethic?" Environmental
      Ethics 3, 4 (Winter 1981) 293-308.

      Criticized is the recommendation of many economists that
      land use regulations should stimulate what markets would,
      were all resources fully owned and freely exchanged. This
      "efficiency" approach, even when balanced with equity
      considerations, is argued to result in commercial sprawl, an
      environment that consumers pay for, but one that appalls
      ethical judgment and aesthetic taste. Economic strategies
      intended to avoid this result are shown to be inadequate,
      and it is concluded that ethical and aesthetic as well as
      economic principles are needed to guide land use policies.

257. Schubert, Jr., Glendon A. "'The Public Interest' in
      Administrative Decision-Making: Theorem, Theosophy, or
      Theory?" American Political Science Review 51 (June
      1957) 346-368.

      Schubert summarizes the prevalent "public interest"
      theories at the time by assigning them to one of three
      schools: "Administrative Rationalism," "Administrative
      Platonism," and "Administrative Realism." Describing these
      categories as unsatisfactory or inadequate, he sides with
      those who favor more modeling and empirically oriented
      investigation of the administrative or "decision-making"
      process.

258. Simon, Herbert A. "Decision-Making and Administrative
      Organization." Public Administration Review 4, 1 (Winter
      1944) 16-30.

      Assuming that within certain limits, each member of an
      organization has some discretion in choosing his or her
      premises for decision making, Simon examines how the

organizational structure influences the selection of these
factual and ethical premises.

259. Still, Jonathan W. "Political Equality and Election
      Systems." (Symposium: Theory and Practice of
      Representation) Ethics 91, 3 (April 1981) 375-394.

      Still examines definitions of political equality and
      finds them lacking in analytical rigor, precision and their
      relation to the institutional mechanisms of electoral
      systems. He then suggests and discusses six criteria that
      must be satisfied before an electoral process can be said to
      provide political equality. These are: (1) universal equal
      suffrage, (2) equal shares, (3) equal probabilities, (4)
      anonymity, (5) majority rule, and (6) proportional group
      representation. The article then discusses applications of
      these criteria in election systems through an examination of
      Supreme Court decisions and proposed constitutional
      amendments that relate to the proposed criteria.

260. Subramaniam, V. "Fact and Value in Decision-Making." Public
      Administration Review 23, 3 (1963) 232-237.

      A review of the major arguments about the "fact-value"
      distinction in decision-making with particular focus on
      Simon's work as the basis for the presentation of a
      "perfect, rational" decision-making model combining facts
      and values to the usual consideration of the means-end
      chain.

261. Thayer, Frederick C. "Values, Truth, and Administration:
      God and Mammon?" Public Administration Review 40, 1
      (January-February 1980) 91-98.

      While providing a review of ten recent (1978 and 1979)
      books on ethics, values, and administration, Thayer actually
      has provided a broad, evaluative essay in which he concludes
      that the continuing problem is really one of conflict
      between authoritative determination of values and humanistic
      determination of values through social processes.

262. Thompson, Dennis F. "The Ethics of Social Experimentation:
      The Case of the DIME." Public Policy 29, 3 (Summer 1981)
      369-398.

      Major ethical issues that arise in social experiments
      conducted by the government are considered. By examining
      the history of one experiment, the 20-year program in the

Denver Income Maintenance Experiment (DIME), some general
criteria are developed for determination of whether to
initiate such experiments. These criteria fall into two
general categories: the consequences of the experiment, and
the consent of persons affected by the experiment. Also
discussed is the basis of commitments that governments make
to citizens who participate in social experiments; the
conditions under which such commitments might be overridden
are analyzed. While the DIME did not fully satisfy the
ethical criteria for an acceptable social experiment, future
experiments are more likely to do so if government officials
consider ethical criteria more deliberately when initiating
and terminating the experiments.

263. Toulmin, Stephen. "The Tyranny of Principles." The
      Hastings Center Report 11, 6 (December 1981) 31-39.

      In an overreaction to a perceived moral relativism
developed in the course of sociocultural research, there has
been a strengthening of inflexible, absolutist positions on
ethics in attitudes toward justice, politics, and public
administration. The finding of a new "tyranny of general
principles" is examined, based on participant observation,
in the debate on research using human subjects, the abortion
debate, and the harsh, arbitrary, decision making in the
administration of social welfare benefits. An historical
account of the role of rules in legal practice and public
administration is provided, showing the tendency of
principles to become more rigid with bureaucratic growth.
In human practice, ethics must be used with a view toward
situational factors.

264. Truelson, Judith. "Blowing the Whistle on Systemic
      Corruption." Ph.D. Dissertation, University of Southern
      California, 1986.

      As the first empirical analysis of intense retaliation
against legitimate whistleblowing in large organizations,
this research moves beyond analysis of individual
whistleblowers' motivations to focus on the institutional
dynamics of the interaction among individual whistleblowers,
organizations, and their environments.

      This study draws upon the theoretical framework of
systemic corruption--an organized conspiracy to suppress
revelation of corrupt practices--to propose a retaliation
model to account for organizational retaliation against
whistleblowers with legitimate protests.

This study analyzes the retaliation model in terms of the relationship between the dependent variables of intensity of organizational retaliation against whistleblowers, the intensity of the whistleblowing process and the whistleblower's role influence, the intervening variable of legal and other supports used by the whistleblower to combat retaliation; and, the independent variables merit of the whistleblower's issue, and organizational size.

Cases of organizational retaliation against legitimate whistleblowing were drawn from an established whistleblower database and were documented in relation to the study variables through a comprehensive review of relevant literature and court cases. Selected, partially structured interviews were also conducted. Using the methodology of negative case analysis—derived from John Stuart Mill's "method of difference," based on the assumption that a perfect form of scientific knowledge is universal generalization —40 cases (plus, for purposes of proof, 2 cases involving intense retaliation in small organizations) were compared against a preliminary hypothesis.

Revisions to the preliminary hypothesis suggest that the more serious the whistleblower's issue, the more the whistleblower needs to seek strong political and legal supports to combat the expected intensity of organizational retaliation against whistleblowing. Yet, successful whistleblowing in a corrupt system appears unlikely. The results of this study indicate that the organizational role influence of all whistleblowers under study was totally or essentially eliminated, while none of the whistleblowers affected organizational reform of their protest issues.

265. Wachs, Martin. "Ethical Dilemmas in Forecasting for Public Policy." Public Administration Review 42, 6 (November-December 1982) 562-567.

Forecasting is shown to possess an ethical dimension for those public policy makers who, of necessity, must use and make them. Forecasts and forecasting utilize the language of, and thus assume the color of, technical objectivity; yet so many technical assumptions are necessary in the construction of a forecast that the process is actually very subjective. In that process, what is actually true can become obscured, unintentionally or otherwise. A forecast is by nature unverifiable; it is largely determined by its assumptions, however cast, and is a technically difficult

act revealing its results but not its mechanisms or
assumptions. Illusions of objectivity and ethical conduct
are supported by those technical experts who make forecasts,
those advocates for a particular position who build a case
on "objective data" and those politicians who accept such
data without questioning; when direct charges have been
made, rarely has the forecast or the forecasting process
been indicated—a further extension of the illusion. Issues
of advocacy and objectivity, data selection, technique, the
forecasting context, and the verifications and implications
of the ethical considerations presented are examined in
detail.

266. Weale, Albert P. "Representation, Individualism, and
      Collectivism." Ethics 91 (April 1981) 457-465.

      The author is concerned with the ethical implications of
democracy. He argues that a theory of representation should
seek to answer three questions: Who is to be represented?
What is to be represented? And how is the representation to
take place? Liberal individualism answers each of these
questions in a distinctive way. In answer to the question
"who?" it replies that individual persons are the subject of
representation; and in answer to the question "what?" that
an individual's view of his or her own interests is
paramount, so that his or her wants or preferences should
form the stuff of representation. The answer to the
question "how?" is slightly more complicated, but its
essence is to say that the representation should take place
by means of a social choice mechanism that is as responsive
as possible to variations in individual preference. The
purpose of this comment is to see how far this theory can be
applied to the problems. I suggest that a collect-
ivist, rather than an individualist theory of
representation is needed to solve these problems.

267. Weisband, Edward, and Thomas M. Frank. Resignation in
      Protest: Political and Ethical Choices Between Loyalty
      to Team and Loyalty to Conscience in American Public
      Life. New York: Grossman (1975).

      The authors use ad hoc examples, case studies, and some
quantitative data to support their argument that there are
significant social benefits as well as costs resulting from
individual action in the face of conflicting social values.
They advocate the importance of an individual's "ethical
autonomy" even while acknowledging that such autonomy does
not guarantee the correctness or acceptance of such a

decision.

This book is about the individual at the breaking point.
It is about protest resignations compelled by unbearable
misgivings; about men and women who disagree with what they
see going on around them in the labyrinths of power and who
resign in order to be free to tell their story.

It is also about top officials who disagree profoundly
with key government policies, but who keep silent, placing
loyalty to the team or careerism ahead of loyalty to
principle and to the public. It is about men and women in
power who wrestle mightily with their consciences—and win.

And, since silent acquiescence, getting along, became so
much the order of the day in government, this book examines
the costs of a system based above all on the value of "team
play." Men and women in places of power and responsibility
who choose not to pay the price of personal integrity merely
succeed in shifting those costs to society as a whole.

268. Yesley, Michael S. "The Ethics Advisory Board and the Right
      to Know." The Hastings Center Report 10, 5 (October
      1980) 5-9.

Bioethical decision making has come to occupy much
attention at institutional and national levels. The field
is still an emerging one, however, with substantial
uncertainty and controversy surrounding the processes of
decision making no less than the actual conclusions of
ethical review. Analyzed are consideration and resolution
of two issues by a federal ethical review body (the Ethics
Advisory Board of the Department of Health, Education, and
Welfare) as part of a broader investigation of the
appropriate function of such a group. Particular focus is
on the interrelationship between facts and values in the
resolution of ethical conflicts. It is concluded that the
role of an ethical review body does not begin and end with
the application of moral principles, but the consideration
of factual material as well as moral evaluation will
normally be required. The unique qualification of a review
body with diverse membership is its ability to examine
difficult issues from a very broad perspective, which may be
the essence of an "ethical" approach.

Chapter IX

Case Study Applications

269. Bertozzi, Mark. <u>Oversight of the Executive Branch: A</u>
     <u>Policy Analysis of Federal Special Prosecutor</u>
     <u>Legislation.</u> Ph.D. Dissertation, State University of New
     York at Albany (1980).

     The events of the Watergate era resulted in an extensive
     body of proposals for the establishment of a Federal Special
     Prosecutor for the purpose of investigating and prosecuting
     government crimes. The Special Prosecutor provisions of the
     Ethics in Government Act of 1978 represent the legislative
     culmination of a major Watergate reform proposed by the
     Ervin Committee. Despite the great promise with which
     Special Prosecutor legislation was initiated, there is
     considerable evidence that the current Special Prosecutor
     law fails to correct problems in the administration of
     justice that provided justification for its enactment.

     This dissertation is an analysis of Federal Special
     Prosecutor legislation and the current Special Prosecutor
     provisions of the Ethics in Government Act. Major
     components of the analysis are as follows: (a) The
     theoretical issues raised by the proposed establishment of a
     Federal Special Prosecutor are explored. Emphasis is given
     to how these issues are used to construct the policy area in
     which the development of the Special Prosecutor legislation
     took place; (b) A comprehensive depiction and
     categorization of the spectrum of Special Prosecutor models
     is presented. Many are shown to be related through shared
     sponsorship or relevant historical episode; (c) Major
     "policy" considerations concerning the establishment and
     operation of a Federal Special Prosecutor are analyzed.
     These matters of policy were crucial in attempting to select
     effective and politically viable design components; (d) The
     operation of the current Special Prosecutor law is explained
     and analyzed. Evidence is presented that it fails to remove
     the Attorney General from the appearance of conflict of
     interest in government crimes and may further politicize his
     role as chief law enforcer; (e) The dissertation
     establishes criteria for an effective Special Prosecutor
     mechanism. It is conclusive with regard to the strongest
     proposals and their most effective design components. It
     provides a recommendation for salvaging the "temporary"
     Special Prosecutor mechanism as an effective investigative
     and prosecutive device.

270. Dann, C. Marshall. "Ethics in Government Act of 1978."
     <u>Journal of Patent Office Society</u> 62 (December 1980)
     721-731.

The article is an attempt to dispel some of the confusion
and misunderstanding surrounding the new ethic legislation.
This article is designed to provide a better comprehension
of the legislative restrictions. The article reviews the
pre- and post-law ethics practices for employees in the
Patent and Trade Office.

271. Dryfoos, Paul (ed). Cases in Public Policy and Management.
      Boston: Boston University (1984) 21-25.

      This is an annotated bibliography of 22 cases designed to
      develop student skills in identifying and analyzing ethical
      and moral issues facing administrators in the public and
      nonprofit sectors. The articles include a wide range of
      issues that a contemporary administrator might face.
      Included in these would be International security, financial
      management, legislative issues, occupational safety,
      government regulation, corporate responsibility and
      community relations.

272. Hudson, James L. "The Ethics of Immigration Restriction."
      Social Theory and Practice 10, 2 (Summer 1984) 201-239.

      A discussion of moral arguments in favor of governmental
      restrictions on immigration for the protection of: (1)
      domestic wage levels; (2) citizens' sensibilities, which
      would be irritated by contact with undesirable ethnic
      groups; (3) institutions of the welfare state; and (4)
      domestic order and justice. All except a heavily qualified
      version of (4) are found wanting. As for (4), conditions
      are specified under which a politically powerful group in
      one country may justifiably impose immigration restrictions
      to defend itself against prospective injustices. Use is
      made of common sense ethical intuitions, supplemented with
      analogies between immigration restriction and governmentally
      imposed birth control, racial discrimination, and preventive
      detention; utilitarian calculations are also sketched. It
      is concluded that immigration restrictions are very seldom
      morally justified.

273. Jack, Louis Bernard. "Constitutional Aspects of Financial
      Disclosure Under the Ethics in Government Act." Catholic
      University Law Review 30 (Summer 1981) 583-603.

      This article is an analysis of the legal aspects of the
      Ethics in Government Act of 1978 as it relates to high level
      federal officials who must make public disclosure of their

personal finances and finances of their spouses and
dependent children. The author concludes that mandatory
financial disclosure may be legislated in a constitutionally
permissible fashion.

274. James, Sharon Kay. A Study of Ethical Attitudes Toward
      Communication Acts in American Society. Ph.D.
      Dissertation, University of Kansas (1982).

      The 1970s produced a crisis in values. Behaviors in
      general, and communication behaviors in particular, became
      suspect.

      This study explored the ethical attitudes of five
      population groups--business, military, government,
      journalism, and the general public--toward the communication
      acts of lying and control of information. Data was
      collected through historical and survey methods.

      Four basic conclusions were drawn from the study. First,
      we live in a pluralistic society where our major professions
      differ in their ethical attitudes toward lying and control
      of information. Second, professions which have established
      specific codes of ethical conduct (military, government, and
      journalism) expressed attitudes congruent with the codes.
      Third, contemporary organizational demands and structures
      may force behaviors incongruent with expressed ethical
      attitudes. Fourth, one of the major challenges for our
      society may be the reconciling of both the teleological and
      deontological approaches to ethics. We do not necessarily
      live in an unethical society, but rather a society where the
      ends and means of behavior are treated differently in
      various ethical systems. In this study, the general public
      and business disapproved of lying, and the general public
      and journalism disapproved of lenient control of
      information; presumably, the disapproval depended on
      judgment of the ends of the action. On the other hand,
      military and government consistently expressed the strongest
      disapproval of lying and lenient control of information,
      perhaps reflecting the deontological concept of "one must
      always follow the moral rule."

275. Kent, Jr., James D. Conflicting Loyalties Among
      Professionals on Leg.slative Staffs: The Case of Program
      Evaluation. D.P.A. Dissertation, State University of New
      York at Albany (1983).

      Conflict between loyalty to an employer and loyalty to a

particular set of ethics is regarded as legitimate if one is practicing a recognized "profession." If legislative program evaluation (LPE) is or can become a "professional" endeavor, the implications of its being part of the legislative process may be considerable.

Two case studies are used to determine how patterns suggested by earlier findings are manifested in actual situations. Results suggest agreement on measurements of quality of LPE work, and also on the need for professional-type independence in the course of the LPE inquiry.

It is concluded that LPE seems to have elements of both an academic-style profession and a journalistic one. Demands for independence by LPE practitioners may clash with legislators' need for political sensitivity. Legislators may find they cannot deal comfortably with this potentially influential group of employees. They may then decide to discontinue LPE staff work or to develop decision-making patterns which rely less heavily on LPE results.

276. McGee, Francis P., and Capt. Francis J. Anzelmi. "There is No Such Thing as a Free Ride." Public Personnel Management 10, 1 (1981).

This article relates a situation which focuses on a developing relationship between a public service professional and a businessman. The article centers on the implications of their relationship, particularly in mixing friendship with the world of work and potential pitfalls that may occur. The article provides a "real world" care study and analysis.

277. Penbera, Joseph J. "Bayview Civic Center." Public Personnel Management 10, 1 (1981).

This article focuses on ethical problems faced by the administration of a for profit, semi-autonomous civic center. The dilemma facing the City of Bayview involved an ethical conflict over how the public interest is best served and to what extent if any should economic objectives of the Civic Center supersede the basic social purposes of other city departments.

278. Sundquist, James L. "Reflections on Watergate: Lessons for Public Administration." Public Administration Review 34, 5 (September-October 1974) 453-461.

Adapted from a lecture at Syracuse University, this essay suggests that the President be subject to congressional removal through a process resembling a "no-confidence" vote rather than the existing impeachment process. Sundquist believes that public administrators must accept guilt as well as others for the conditions and climate leading to Watergate.

279. Tifft, Larry. "Capital Punishment Research, Policy, and Ethics: Defining Murder and Placing Murderers." Crime and Social Justice 17 (Summer 1982) 61-68.

An analytical framework is outlined to explore the meaning of the capital punishment debate and capital punishment as public policy. Reviewing research in this area, it is concluded that the public policy of execution arises in the context wherein life is cheap, surplus, and not an end in itself. Capital punishment discourse and executions arise in the context of a call for more severe and ceremonious exercises of power, a stronger centralized state, and a clearer reinforcement of the base values of hierarchy and authority. The execution reproduces and dramatizes the acceptance of the exercise of power; the state, in responding to "murder," increases its legitimate exercise of power in other forms of death-dealing. Capital punishment and its discourse also produce ignorance; excluded from the discourse are the necessity and desirability of having an ethical social order wherein death-dealing is absent and the exercise of power transformed and dissolved.

280. Usher, Ronald L. "The Myth of the Monterey Mafia." Public Personnel Management 10, 1 (1981).

This article is a narrative discussion of events surrounding the hiring activities of the city manager. The article relates the personnel activities of how to deal with rumors of impropriety.

281. Walter, J. Jackson. "The Ethics in Government Act, Conflict of Interest Laws and Presidential Recruiting." Public Administration Review 41 (November-December 1981) 659-665.

An exploration of the affect of the Ethics in Government Act of 1978 in the recruiting of leaders for the Executive Branch. The author follows a detailed description of the

requirements of the statute, the processes that have been
developed to implement it, and prospective remedies for
potential problems. Jackson concludes that the criticism of
the Ethics Act, as it relates to recruiting barriers, has
been imprecise and somewhat misleading. He cites prevailing
compensation levels and the decreased quality of public life
as other factors impeding the recruitment of high level
executives. An excellent description of the process engaged
in to review a candidate's financial disclosure forms for
potential conflicts of interest is a strength of this
article.

Chapter X

Competing Paradigms and Theoretical Frameworks

282. Bardes, Barbara A., and Melvin J. Dubnick. "Motives and
      Methods in Policy Analysis." Improving Policy Analysis
      Stuart S. Nagel (ed). Beverly Hills: Sage Publications
      (1980) 101-127.

      The author's concern is the nature of Public Policy
      Analysis as a field of inquiry. The questions
      central to their investigation are why do social scientists
      and others engage in policy analysis and how do they
      accomplish their tasks? The one fundamental question they
      raise is what qualities are central to the many approaches
      of policy analysis?

283. Brady, F. Neil. "Ethical Theory for the Public
      Administrator: The Management of Competing Interests."
      American Review of Public Administration 15, 2 (Summer
      1981) 119-126.

      An examination is made of the two major ethical theories
      currently utilized in relation to management of competing
      interests by a public administrator. The current theories
      considered are: 1) John Rawls' Kantianism, working in the
      abstract, apart from a specific concrete situation; and 2)
      Classical utilitarianism, concentrating on specific human
      expectations within a given ethical context. In the case of
      the management of competing interests, the utilitarian
      theory falls short because an exclusively utilitarian
      approach would not sufficiently resolve a conflict in which
      special interest groups make unreasonable demands. Instead,
      the administrator must make some prior ethical decisions
      before applying utilitarian theory.

284. Brown, Peter G. "Ethics and Public Policy: A Preliminary
      Agenda." Policy Studies Journal 7, 1 (Autumn 1978)
      132-137.

      This essay examines the future of the developing field of
      ethics and public policy. An overview of descriptive and
      normative ethics is given and four areas of ethical analysis
      in public policy development and evaluation are explored:
      1) The personal ethical problems faced by individual public
      officials; 2) The evaluation of professional practices from
      a public policy standpoint; 3) The analysis of ethical
      assumptions in analytical frameworks; 4) Ethical criteria
      for examining public problems, programs, and alternative
      policy models. What is needed is the development of
      mid-range ethical principles and moral theories developed
      with informed consent to use in appraising public programs.

285. Callahan, Daniel, and Bruce Jennings. Ethics, the Social
     Sciences, and Policy Analysis. New York: Plenum (1982).

     The author addresses the proper role of ethics, social
     science   and   policy   making,   and   offers   ethical
     guidelines pertinent to the practice of policy analysis and
     applied social research. One section of the book is devoted
     to key ethical problems raised by the relationship between
     social science and policy. The authors challenge
     researchers to be ethically sensitive to their work.

286. Care, Norman S. "Participation and Policy." Ethics 88, 4
     (July 1978) 316-337.

     Proponents of political democracy are in a dilemma
     concerning the morally acceptable policies for a community.
     Two possible reactions are the settlement and convergence
     views. The convergence, or solution from participation,
     thesis is explored, finding that all but four of the
     following conditions must be satisfied by persons involved
     in strong participation: 1) noncoercion; 2) rationality;
     3) acceptance of terms; 4) disinterestedness; 5) joint
     agreement;   6)   universality;   7)   community
     self-interestedness;   8) equal and full information;   9)
     nonriskiness; 10) possibility;   11) count all votes;   12)
     voice. Strong participation may not be practical, but it
     can stand as a moral ideal for political practice.

287. Catron, Bayard Lacey. Theoretical Aspects of Social Action:
     Reason, Ethics, and Public Policy. Ph.D. Dissertation,
     University of California, Berkeley (1975).

     This is a work in social theory which attempts to clear
     the ground and lay the groundwork for a systematic
     praxeology, and theory of social practice. It focuses on
     man-as-actor, and develops the undeniable experience of
     intentional action from both a theoretical and practical
     concern. The principal emphasis of the thesis relates to
     public policy--and decision making, planning, and
     administration in the public sector. But the basic concern
     is quite general, embracing as well artists and scientists
     and citizens--and all those for whom prospective action is
     problematic. "Action," then, is an essential term in
     characterizing and understanding human experience.

     The concept of "rational action" is reviewed critically,
     and "practical reason" is defended and developed by means of

a systematic parallel with "theoretical reason." It is suggested that the primary concern of all actors is with right action—in several senses, including "correct," "prudent," and "moral." While the ethical dimension of human action is not thoroughly developed, it is argued that an adequate praxeology must specify its relation to the cognate concerns of ethics and axiology.

The thesis is concerned with the theory of social practice, and also—equally and reciprocally—with the "practice of social theory." The relationship between theory and practice (or praxis) is a central theme throughout. Three pairs of relations are presented and discussed: thinking/acting, theory/practice, and social science/public policy. These pairs and their interrelations are used in an argument that thinking/acting is an incontrovertible unity which, mutatis mutandis, illustrates the fundamental interrelation of theory and practice—which in turn has important implications for the relation between knowledge and action, or social science as applied to public policy. A number of views of the relation of social science and public policy are discussed, and the inadequacy of certain conventional views is revealed in a dialogue between several social scientists and two policy actors.

288. Cawley, Clifford Comer. A Political Philosophy for Today. Ph.D. Dissertation, University of Oregon (1981).

This dissertation's problem is to construct a new political philosophy to cope with today's mounting crises.

The construction proceeds by: (1) analyzing today's alarming condition; (2) taking theological, metaphysical and epistemological stands; (3) hypothesizing man's nature; (4) taking an ethical stand; (5) postulating man's highest possibilities; (6) specifying the institutions accordingly required; (7) defining the political problem of making all this so; and (8) offering a possible solution.

Results are summarized as follows: (1) Man's annihilation by war is possible within the next hour, his suicide by unchecked multiplication and pollution is already well under way, and non-manmade cosmic or terrestrial annihilation is possible at any time; (2) Natural and revealed theologies are rejected, the possibility of an indifferent creator conceded. Urgency dictates acceptance of a material, if fuzzy-edged reality—an Als Ob, Pascal-like truce with metaphysics—and an epistemology between Locke and Hume; (3) With the advent of mammals, primal greed was overlaid with the instinct for family survival: man added altruism. Now, no limits exist to man's continuing, intelligence-directed genetic and social evolution and to the evolution of intelligence itself; (4) With present "good" intentions leading to disaster, ethical systems based on revelation or natural law are rejected. Adopted is a pragmatic new ethics designed to assure mankind's survival and continued evolution; (5) Understanding his origin, man can design his future. Survival dictates the conquest and colonization of space—and this will require coming so close to "knowing everything" as to win him at least a permanent place in the universe, if not some say in its running; (6) To mount the conceptual and technological effort required for that conquest, and first to negate the war and numbers threats, requires a world government; (7) The political problem therefore is how to impose a sovereign world government upon eight-score independent States—and fast. (8) Proposed is a world government built out from the invincible nucleus of a China-America-Russia federation—CHAMRU; this merger to be engineered by an American third party after its winning to power on that platform.

289. Clohesy, William Warren. Kant and the Cultivation of Freedom. Ph.D. Dissertation, New School for Social Research (1981).

Kant's moral philosophy looks upon the agent's motivation as the sole standard according his actions moral worth. An action is moral because one acts from awareness that the moral law ought to be obeyed. This point, central to Kant's thought, is the source of much criticism: Is it a matter of moral indifference what a person recognizes as his duty?

The intention of this dissertation is to present a reading of Kant's practical thought which focuses upon the purposive structure and regulative ideas, so that his arguments and concepts, perplexing in isolation, form a coherent whole as a vision of mankind's proper moral destiny.

The first chapter considers the importance of the Copernican Revolution for a practical world emergent within the spatio-temporal world of science. Kant accepts the scientific world view, but he also recognizes that men must make of the universe a world of their own. The second chapter shows the insufficiency of any empirical goods as the ground of morality. For Kant all empirical ethics are but dreams of goods for one's own happiness. The third chapter considers freedom as binding oneself to laws of one's own making in both its modes--personal autonomy and political liberty. Kant is allied in his concept of freedom with Montesquieu and Rousseau against the Liberalism of Hobbes and Locke. Men are capable of dispassionate acts, personally and politically. The fourth and fifth chapters enlarge upon Kant's vision, based upon the arguments of the first three chapters.

The conclusion offers a summary of the dissertation's presentation of Kant's purpose in his practical philosophy: to assure men of the powers they can and ought to cultivate for themselves.

290. Dunn, William N. "Values, Ethics, and Standards in Policy Analysis." Encyclopedia of Policy Studies Stuart S. Nagel (ed). New York: Marcel Dekker (1982).

291. Dunn, William N. (ed). Values, Ethics, and the Practice of Policy Analysis. Lexington, Mass: D.C. Heath and Company (1983).

Policy analysis has tended to overlook and neglect the questions of values and ethics. This book seeks to correct this shortcoming by bringing together a cross-section of contributions that focus on a central question: How do personal, professional, social values, and ethics affect the practice of policy analysis? The book focuses on the diversity of personal, professional, social values, and ethics among planners, policy analysts, and public managers. The chapters address common problems, issues, and themes. In addition, they provide a forum to enlarge our ethical knowledge and practice of policy analysis.

292. Eimicke, William B. Public Administration in a Democratic Context: Theory and Practice. Sage Professional Papers in Administrative and Policy Studies, 2 (1974).

An examination of the problems of the bureaucracy within the framework of American democracy, Eimicke concludes that neither faith in man's ultimate morality nor specific reforms in response to bureaucratic problems will suffice--seeking a balance between the two must come through popular control.

293. Emmitt, Robert Joseph. <u>Scientific Humanism and Liberal Education: The Philosophy of Jacob Bronowski</u>. Ph.D. Dissertation, University of Southern California (1982).

The Scientific Humanism of the late Jacob Bronowski (1908-1974) is considered as a philosophical system and as a basis for a twentieth century liberal arts curriculum that gives equal emphasis to arts, science, and ethics. The philosophy is examined for unity, consistency, and comprehensiveness as a contemporary philosophy of knowledge and proposed as an alternative to the Neo-Thomist philosophy of liberal education advanced by Robert Maynard Hutchins and Mortimer Adler.

Two previous dissertations on Bronowski have failed to consider his philosophy as a coherent whole or to examine his ideas or their educational implications in depth. By means of extensive structural and textual comparisons, Bronowski's philosophy is shown to have a strong Neo-Kantian component, and a particular affinity with the humanism of Kant's later writings on esthetics, society and government, anthropology and education in The Critique of Judgment, Idea for a Universal History, and Anthropology. There are also significant, though less extensive, associations with the scientific and mathematical ideas in the Critique of Pure Reason, and with pragmatism, conventionalism, and constructivism.

Bronowski's philosophy is distinguished from Kant's by its integration of modern concepts of relativity, uncertainty, and evolution; by the accession of a vast store of contemporary mathematical, physical, and biological evidence; and by its vision of a more complex immanent and evolving unity of science, art, and ethics. Perhaps the most striking of many improvements in the Kantian synthesis is the derivation of an ethical imperative directly from the epistemology of science and scholarship.

Both traditional and original elements are incorporated into Bronowski's proposals for a core liberal arts curriculum. It is concluded that Bronowski not only developed a unified philosophy of knowledge that can stand on contemporary foundations, but also one that can support a broad program of liberal education on a basis superior to Neo-Thomism in its inherent commitment to modern democracy, science, and ethics, and in its freedom from sectarian metaphysics.

294. Finkle, Arthur L. "A Discipline in Search of Legitimacy."
      Bureaucrat 13, 2 (Summer 1984) 58-60.

      The article discusses the efforts of public
      administration as a discipline seeking legitimacy,
      self-respect, standards, and definition of goals, purposes,
      pursuits, and policies. The case for licensing of
      practitioners is discussed explicitly. Included is a code
      of ethics for the American Society for Public
      Administration.

295. Gawthrop, Louis C. "Administrative Responsibility: The
      Systems State and Our Wilsonian Legacy." Public
      Administration and Public Policy H. George Frederickson
      and Charles R. Wise (eds.); Lexington, Mass.; D.C. Heath
      and Co. (1977).

      As information and evaluation relies more in the future
      on general systems theory and techniques, Gawthrop argues
      that traditional ideas of what constitutes "ethical"
      problems for public administrators will have to be rethought
      to include a consideration of issues beyond the legalistic
      orientation of the past and present. He suggests movement
      toward an "antiopatory" consideration of issues within the
      context of the individual conscience and its relational
      responsibilities to environmental factors not always clearly
      defined or foreseen.

296. Goodnow, Frank J. Politics and Administration. New York:
      The Macmillan Co. (1900).

      Written in 1900, this book is a classic in American
      Government. Goodnow provides a vivid picture of the
      political condition which existed in the United States at
      the turn of the century. He recognized that the formal
      system set in law may not be the same as the actual system.
      In addition to his discussion of the political system, he
      offers suggestions of how the system might be improved.

297. Gulick, Luther. "Democracy and Administration Face the
      Future." Public Administration Review 37, 6
      (November-December 1977) 706-711.

      In this address to Indiana University's School of Public
      and Environmental Affairs, the author notes a political and
      moral failure in recent public leadership which is leading
      to the betrayal of traditional American values, and argues
      that administrators face fundamental challenges in ethics

and management which must be met. The author identifies such factors as the government's having assumed a positive role out of a negative one, having unjustifiably raised public expectations, having been brought into an era of rapid technological change without environmental support, political corruption, and the astronomic growth in power of private corporations as symptomatic of this failure. The author then turns briefly to the development of sociobiology and argues in conclusion that an organic analogy based on sociobiology can be applied to public administration, and be used to integrate problem solving into a coherent approach to the future.

298. Gulick, Luther.   "Science, Values and Public Administration." Papers on the Science of Administration Luther Gulick, Lyndall Urwick and James D. Mooney (eds.) New York: Institute of Public Administration, Columbia University (1937).

A statement of the position that public administrators need not give up the quest for efficiency simply because "obstacles" such as citizen participation inherent in the value system of a democracy make progress less "exact" than science would seem to dictate.

299. Gunn, Elizabeth.   "Ethics and the Public Service: An Annotated Bibliography and Overview Essay." Public Personnel Management 10, 1 (1981) 172-178.

This article provides an excellent review and analysis of the literature in the field of Ethics and Public Policy. The discussion of the literature is very useful and an important contribution to the study of Public Administration. This is a capstone article to an entire issue which is devoted to ethics.

300. Horwitz, Robert H. (ed).   The Moral Foundations of the American Republic. Charlottesville: University of Virginia Press (1977).

This collection of ten essays grapples with the tension inherent between such concepts as liberty and equality, questions raised regarding the men who wrote and the documents which contained these words, and the implications for a continuing moral base in political society. Essays by Robert A. Goldwin ("Of Men and Angels: A Search for Morality in the Constitution," pp. 1-18), Martin Diamond ("Ethics and Politics: The American Way," pp. 39-72), and

Wilson Carey McWilliams ("On Equality as the Moral Foundation for Community," pp. 183-213) are more relevant than others.

301. Howe, Elizabeth, and Jerome Kaufman. "Ethics and Professional Practice." Values, Ethics, and the Practice of Policy Analysis Dunn (ed). Lexington, Mass: D.C. Heath and Company (1983) 9-32.

Professional ethical principles are oriented either toward the ends or the means of professional behavior. Two major issues of means-oriented ethics for urban and regional planning professionals are examined here: (1) Whether the desired ends should affect the choice of means; and (2) What, if any, are the limits to be observed in the employment of means? Results of a survey of planners' attitudes provide the data for an heirarchical classification of means considered to be most and least ethical. The differences among planners in terms of responses to this hierarchy are discussed. Implications for other areas of public policy are examined.

302. Kaplan, Abraham. American Ethics and Public Policy. New York: Oxford University Press (1963).

Kaplan explores the role of ethics in American politics and policy-making and concludes that morality or ethical behavior must be an ever-present everyday commitment or approach to problem-solving--not just reserved for crises. Public officials must learn when making decisions to merge their idealism or dependence on absolutes with the reality of the choices at hand.

303. Kateb, George. "The Moral Distinctiveness of Representative Democracy." Ethics 91 (April 1981) 357-374.

This article is a part of a special issue devoted to representation, democracy, and political theory. The ethical concern raised by the author is the question of authority, power, and representation. He states that in a representative democracy the sources of law and public policy are a collection of office holders who have attained office by winning elections. Elections provide some general guidance to the winners concerning public opinion and policy preferences. Thus, the fundamental institution of representative democracy is the electoral system.

304. Ladd, John. "Policy Studies and Ethics." Policy Studies
        Journal 2, 1 (1973) 38-43.

        Discusses several ethical issues raised by public policy
        studies; part of a 1973 symposium on "Interdisciplinary
        Approaches to Policy Studies."

305. Lasswell, Harold D., and Harlan Cleveland. The Ethics of
        Power: The Interplay of Religion, Philosophy, and
        Politics. New York: Harper and Brothers (1962).

        A group of essays with comments on themes such as the
        relevance of differing ethical systems for "government,
        politics and administration, the relationship between legal
        and ethical norms, and current normative issues."

306. Longwood, Walter Merle. The Ends of Government in the
        Thought of Reinhold Niebuhr and Jacques Maritain: A
        Study in Christian Social Ethics. Ph.D. Dissertation,
        Yale University (1969).

        This dissertation examines the political thought of
        Reinhold Niebuhr and Jacques Maritain from the perspective
        of the ends of government. The first two chapters are of a
        general nature, analyzing their theories of politics and
        ethics. The last three chapters deal more specifically with
        the moral criteria the authors set forth for evaluating the
        ends or purposes of institutions, laws, or policies.

        The author locates Niebuhr and Maritain within the
        liberal and Aristotelian political traditions, respectively.
        Niebuhr views the political society as a convention which is
        desirable as a means for enabling men to attain their
        individual ends of freedom, whereas Maritain views the
        political society as a natural institution which embodies
        moral values. In examining their theories of ethics, he
        shows how both authors can be interpreted as teleological
        natural law thinkers, the distinction between them being a
        material difference within a formal and fundamental
        agreement. Niebuhr delineates this "law of life" in a much
        more individualistic manner than Maritain does, and this has
        serious consequences for his conception of the relation
        between ethics and politics.

307. MacRae, Jr., Duncan. "Policy Analysis: An Applied Social
        Science Discipline." Administration and Society 6 (1975)
        375-380.

The author argues for a new social science discipline
based on the ethical justification of public policy. The
guidance of social choice and the criticism of expert advice
require reasoned valuative criteria for judgment. In this
article the author is an advocate of an applied social
science discipline based on systematic ethical discourse.
He suggests that the basis for the valuative discourse can
be found in the latent ethics of the social sciences.

308. MacRae, Jr., Duncan. The Social Function of Social Science.
      New Haven: Yale University Press (1976).

309. Mansbridge, Jane J. "Living with Conflict: Representation
      in the Theory of Adversary Democracy." Ethics 91 (April
      1981) 466-476.

The contemporary normative theory of democracy is almost
entirely an "adversary" theory based on the assumption of
conflicting interests among the citizens and conceived
largely as a means of handling that conflict. How close the
members of a polity come to having a common interest on an
issue is the single most important determinant of how much
they need to concern themselves with political equality in
representation.

310. Meyers, Marvin. "The Least Imperfect Government: On Martin
      Diamond's 'Ethics and Politics.'" Interpretation 8, 2/3
      (May 1980) 5-15.

The political philosophy of Martin Diamond is examined in
this article, focusing on the late author's essay on ethics
and politics and the founding of the American Republic.
Diamond's philosophical and intellectual development are
described in the context of his central theme of American
Modernity against the old and ancient. Of special interest
in this article is Diamond's attribution to the Founding
Fathers, of a deliberate design for replacing the ancient
with the modern, and his life-long study of James Madison.

311. Monti, Joseph Ernest. Ethics and Public Policy: The
      Conditions of Public Moral Discourse. Ph.D.
      Dissertation, Vanderbilt University (1981).

The problem addressed in this study is the crisis in the
policy process--a crisis of fragmentation, reductionism, and
isolation among the policy sciences. Such a situation leads
to policies that are formed in the light of vested interests
of the policy sciences themselves, or of social and

political groups who use their recommendations for their own
purposes. This dissertation argues that a new
self-understanding is necessary for the policy process, one
based on a restructuring of the conditions for an adequate
participatory dialogue about policy questions. In fact, the
question for attention becomes an investigation into the
conditions of public moral discourse in general. The
practice of competent public moral discourse will ameliorate
the crisis of fragmentation, reductionism, and isolation
among the policy sciences and will ground a new
participatory ethos for society. Toward this end, the
dissertation suggests ethics, considered as an evaluative
hermeneutic of culture and of history itself, be
reconstituted as the center of the practical moral discourse
of the policy sciences. Policy study, in this
evaluative-hermeneutic form, will be properly public and
dialogical.

Chapter Six returns the argument of the basic problems of
fragmentation, reductionism, and isolation that inhere in
the policy process and the whole of society. With a summary
of the argument, final comparisons with the work of another
analyst of the policy crisis (Duncan MacRae), and a
statement of general implications, the dissertation
concludes.

312. Nagel, Stuart S. (ed). Encyclopedia of Policy Studies. New
      York: Marcel Dekker (1982).

313. Neibuhr, Reinhold. Moral Man and Immoral Society: A Study
      in Ethics and Politics. New York: Charles Scribner's
      Sons (1960).

A conceptual consideration of the implications of "the
basic difference between the morality of individuals and the
morality of collectiveness, whether races, classes, or
nations."

314. Peterson, Susan Rae. "The Compatibility of Richard Price's
      Politics and Ethics." Journal of the History of Ideas
      45, 4 (October-December 1984) 537-547.

Critics of Richard Price (1723-1791), the British
political and moral philosopher, point to the apparent
inconsistency between the emphasis on duty in his ethics and
the stress on liberty in his political thought. In fact,
Price argued that self-determination is a precondition for
moral agency, stating that individuals need liberty both to

exercise their free will as moral agents and to fulfill
their political duties as good citizens. According to
Price, individuals possess the moral and political right to
determine their fate without interference, and a just
government must protect the liberty of its citizens to act
morally. In his work, he anticipated rational intuitionism,
deontological ethics, modern analytic moral philosophy and
ordinary language analysis. He provided a classical
refutation of utilitarianism and an eloquent defense of
civil liberty.

315. Rabin, Jack, Gerald J. Miller, and W. Bartley Hildreth.
      "Administrative Malpractice Suits: Tort Liability and
      the Challenge to Professionalism." Public Personnel
      Management 10, 1 (1981).

Ethical issues serve as the foundation for a public
official's exposure to personal tort liability risks.
Basically, the issue is one of professional ethics, or a set
of internalized norms. A large number of liability suits
have allowed courts to announce that administrative behavior
does not necessarily reflect certain ethical values. In
fact, the courts have had to resurrect a one
hundred-year-old statute (the Civil Rights Act of 1871) to
provide the impetus for confronting malpractice in
government.

The Civil Rights Act of 1871 has forced liability and its
ethical connotations to the forefront of the professional
administrator's agenda. Moreover, the U.S. Congress has
encouraged attorneys to represent these citizens through the
Civil Rights Attorneys Fees Act of 1976. Finally, the
general feeling exists that individuals should turn to the
courts to settle issues that were once resolved in other
forums.

This essay examines the 1871 law and illustrates relevant
ethical dilemmas. We turn first to a brief review of the
basis for personal tort liability suits and other legal
developments which help clarify the public official's
responsibilities. Later, the focus shifts to court-defined,
implicit ethical rules. The essay closes on the impact of
these developments on the issue of professionalism.

316. Rae, Douglas. "Two Contradictory Ideas of (Political)
      Equality." Ethics 91 (April 1981) 451-456.

There are two very different ways of thinking about

equality in general and thus two very different ways of
thinking about political equality (and equal representation)
in particular. The tension between these two views explains
some important problems in the jurisprudence of political
equality, and the eventual irreconcilability of these two
views points toward an ultimate limit on the attainment of
political equality and equal representation. One of the two
egalitarianisms is attainable, and the other is not; one is
sensitive to persons and their differences while the other
is not; the attainable equality is, alas, the insensitive
one. These points all depend upon there being two views of
equality.

317. Rawls, John. A Theory of Justice. Cambridge: The Belknap
      Press of the Harvard University Press (1971).

      Rawls hopes that this book will clarify the "structural
      features of the conception of justice that is implicit in
      the contract tradition" which he believes is "the most
      appropriate moral basis for a democratic society."

318. Regan, Thomas J. Whitehead's Notion of World Consciousness
      (Ethics, Process, Organism). Ph.D. Dissertaton, Fordham
      University (1984).

      This essay attempts to provide a new reading of the
      Whiteheadian philosophical corpus by presenting it in light
      of the notion of world-consciousness. Initially articulated
      in Religion in the Making, in 1926 this notion is shown to
      lend a degree of conceptual cohesiveness to all the later
      writings. In using this term, Whitehead does not mean a
      political or global vision, rather he means an intuitive
      conscious awareness of the unity of value which is achieved
      when diverse elements within experience are harmonized or
      integrated in such a way as to maximize the possibility for
      value realization.

      After exploring the emergence of world-consciousness in
      Whitehead's theory of religion, the essay moves on to ground
      this vision firmly within Whitehead's metaphysics of
      relation. Next, turning to the practical dimensions of
      world-consciousness, Whitehead's theory of education is
      examined as a means of transmitting this vision to future
      generations. Following this, Whitehead's writings on the
      nature and function of the business community and the
      institutions of government are explored in order to show
      concrete ways in which world-consciousness might be fostered
      in society. Finally, the notion of peace is discussed

insofar as it expresses a mature formulation of the notion of world-consciousness.

Throughout the essay a conscious attempt is made to present the development of the notion of world-consciousness on the microscopic level of the individual person and the macroscopic level of society at large. What emerges from the overall discussion is an aesthetically based theory of value which can serve as the foundation for social ethics.

319. Richtor, Anders. "The Existentialist Executive." Public Administration Review 30, 4 (July-August 1970) 415-422.

Suggests that an existentialist orientation could replace family and societal norms as a basis for decision making and action by emphasizing the liberation of the individual and his resulting ability to tolerate differences in others.

320. Rossum, Ralph A. "Government and Ethics: The Constitutional Foundation." Teaching Political Science 11, 3 (Spring 1984) 100-105.

The current interest in government ethics is examined, beginning with the work of Leonard D. White, who was a founder of the study of public administration. White considered administration in the context of the American political order. Ethics must also be considered in this specific framework. As a basis, the justice of the American regime must be assumed. The criterion of ethics must be adherence to the Constitution. It is argued that there is an ongoing tension between restraint of government power as a means of preventing abuses and the need for a strong government capable of safeguarding liberty. The Supreme Court has departed from the Constitution by deciding for political equality and freedom of speech without accountability. Judicial interventions in policy making should be restrained.

321. Scott, William G., and David K. Hart. "Administrative Crisis: The Neglect of Metaphysical Speculation." Public Administration Review 33 (September-October 1973) 415-422.

The authors see the "real crisis created by the exponential growth of technology" as an administrative one in which the role of administrators have become that of determining the best way to achieve scientific and technological progress rather than of mediating between such

progress and the continuing importance of traditional
values.

322. Scott, William G., and David K. Hart. "The Moral Nature of
      Man in Organizations: A Comparative Analysis." Academy
      of Management Journal 14, 2 (June 1971) 241-255.

      Uniting philosophers with administrative theorists (e.g.,
      Hobbes to Taylor, Locke to Mayo, and Rousseau to McGregor),
      this essay (book review) focuses on "the nature of man" and
      the basis for understanding and building administrative
      control systems.

323. Small, Joseph. "Political Ethics." American Behavioral
      Scientist 19, 5 (May-June 1976) 543-566.

      History reflects that Americans are a people in
      transition involved in continually evolving standards of
      performance and principles of government. Beginning shortly
      before the Civil War, the American people have been
      attempting to distinguish between matters of public interest
      and private interest, the essence of political ethics. It
      is in this context that the author suggests that the
      struggle to define ethical standards in American political
      life is being reflected by comparable changes in the
      military service. It is noted that in the current period,
      military officers find themselves no longer isolated from
      the social and political currents of American life. The
      expansion of the military establishment into a managerial
      enterprise has increased the political responsibilities of
      the military officer. Among the new responsibilities is the
      need to be aware of the progress being made in the area of
      political ethics. To trace the expansion of political
      ethics, the author presents a brief account of the
      historical evolution of the American political system and
      presents various analytic studies that point out the
      conflicts of interest in public affairs. Among the
      pertinent examples of unethical conduct is the most recent
      scandal of political kickbacks involving Vice President
      Agnew and the government perversion of Watergate. In
      presenting the survey, the author attempts to point out
      several key factors: that it is part of human condition to
      seek to acquire money and power from the public sector for
      personal gain; yet it is equally evident that the body
      politic has been leaning in the direction to prevent private
      enrichment at public expense. Society is beginning to
      fashion codes of professional conduct and alerting men and
      women in government services as to what is expected. The

public is becoming more perceptive about the significance of "public interest" as opposed to "private enrichment" at public expense.

324. Steinfels, Peter. "The Place of Ethics in Schools of Public Policy." A report from the Hastings Center, Institute of Society, Ethics, and Life Sciences to the Ford Foundation. mimeographed (April 1977).

A summary of findings and recommendations from visits made to ten graduate schools in public policy to investigate the status of ethics as a specific curriculum concern.

325. Waldo, Dwight. Democracy, Bureaucracy and Hypocrisy. Berkeley, CA: Institute of Governmental Studies, University of California, Berkeley (1977).

An essay for the Royer Lecture in Political Economy on May 13, 1976, written by Waldo who has spent a lifetime trying to grasp the ways to reconcile the ideal of democracy with the necessity of bureaucracy yet confesses to be searching still for the normative framework for reconciling the two concepts.

326. Waldo, Dwight. "Development of Theory of Democratic Administration." American Political Science Review 46 (March 1952) 81-103.

Assuming that "the central meaning of democracy" lies "in an ethic, a set of values," Waldo uses a contrast of the development of public administration with that of private administrative theory to wrestle with the conflict betwen democracy and the need for authority. See his Democracy, Bureaucracy, and Hypocrisy for a more recent treatment of this theme.

327. Wilson, Woodrow. "The Study of Administration." Political Science Quarterly 2 (June 1887) 197-222.

Wilson's essay is usually cited as the origin of the politics-administration dichotomy. Although Wilson's general purpose was to call attention to administration in the public sector as a worthwhile field of study, his distinction between politics and the field of administration had a major impact on later studies of public administration.

328. Young, Fredric Clifton. <u>On Moral Equivalency, Duties, and</u>
       <u>the State: A Study in Social Philosophy</u>. Ph.D.
       Dissertation, University of California, Santa Barbara
       (1981).

       Many philosophers suppose that a breach of a negative
duty is far worse than a breach of a positive duty. Many
moral thinkers hold, for example, that killing someone is
more blameworthy than letting him die. This alleged
asymmetry between negative and positive duties is often
extended to cases of lying vs. withholding of vital
information, etc. If there is such a moral inequality
between negative and positive duties, this inequality may
have farreaching consequences for business ethics, medical
ethics, political philosophy, and so on. It may be a
consequence of such an inequality thesis that advertisers do
less wrong by omitting information than by lying to
consumers, doctors do less wrong in omitting life-saving
treatment than by injecting lethal doses of pain-killing
medicines to their patients, governments do no wrong by only
prosecuting those who breach their negative duties (e.g.,
thieves and murderers), and not those who breach their
positive duties (e.g., so-called Bad Samaritans).

       In this dissertation, the author challenges the view that
there is a moral inequality between negative and positive
duties, and, first considering the clear case of killing and
letting die, show that there is no moral difference, as
such, between negative and positive duties. The author
argues that there is no hard-and-fast metaphysical
distinction between killing and letting die, no causal
difference, and that it is no worse morally to breach the
one kind of duty than it is to breach the other kind.

       This moral equivalency thesis, as referred to, also has
farreaching consequences for business ethics, medical
ethics, and political philosophy. We may have to assert
that if one were to try to sell a product and maliciously
withheld vital information from the customer, one would be
behaving just as badly, all things being considered, as if
one were to deliberately lie about the condition of the
product. We may have to, as well, abolish the distinction
between active and passive euthanasia.

       In the final chapter, the author addresses the concern of
some philosophers that an equality in strictness between
positive and negative duties has the consequence that we may
restrict individual liberty in ways unacceptable to moral

agents. In so doing, the author devotes some time to the
evaluation of the compatibility of Nozick's minimal state
with the moral equivalency thesis. He believes in and
argues for such a compatibility.

329. "Watergate: Its Implications for Responsible Government."
      National Academy of Public Administration Washington,
      D.C.: NAPA (March 1974).

      "A report prepared...at the request of the Senate Select
      Committee on Presidential Campaign Activities" evaluating
      and making recommendations on a wide range of issues raised
      by Watergate both for the American system of government in
      general and for individuals serving in varying capacities
      within the system. Though ethics are given only slight
      coverage (pp. 135-139) in a direct sense, the entire report
      reflects the Academy's concern for improving the integrity
      of the public service.

330. "1977 PAR Conference: 'Ethics of Government.'" PAR
      Analysis 222 (April 1977).

      Summaries of speeches given during the conference address
      such topics as the role of the press and the courts, the
      need for a more restrictive code of ethics, better
      enforcement of existing regulations on financial disclosure
      and lobbying, and education of public officials. Keynote
      address is by former U.S. Senator Sam J. Ervin, Jr.

Chapter XI

Author Index